Improve your Skill

Writing *for IELTS*

with Answer Key

6.0–7.5

Stephanie Dimond-Bayir

MACMILLAN

Macmillan Education
4 Crinan Street
London N1 9XW

A division of Macmillan Publishers Limited

Companies and representatives throughout the world

ISBN 978-0-230-46336-3 (with key)
ISBN 978-0-230-46346-2 (without key)
ISBN 978-0-230-46340-0 (with key + MPO Pack)
ISBN 978-0-230-46338-7 (without key + MPO Pack)

Text, design and illustration © Macmillan Publishers Limited 2014
Written by Stephanie Dimond-Bayir
The author has asserted her right to be identified as the author of this work in accordance
with the Copyright, Designs and Patents Act 1988.

First published 2014

Designed by Kamae Design, Oxford
Illustrated by Kamae Design, p7, 8, 9, 13, 16, 24, 25, 29, 31, 32, 34, 37, 39, 41, 45, 46, 47, 49, 53,
54, 56, 59, 61, 63, 69, 70, 71, 72, 74, 77, 79, 85.
Cover design by Macmillan
Cover photograph by Getty Images/Nicolas Hansen
Picture research by Susannah Jayes

Author's acknowledgements
The author would like to thank Ata, Patricia and Derek and the students of Bell.

The publishers would like to thank all those who participated in the development of the
project, with special thanks to the freelance editor.

The author and publishers would like to thank the following for permission to reproduce their
photographs:

Alamy/Jonathan Cole p84, Alamy/dbimages p54(a), Alamy/epa european pressphoto agency
b.v. p30(b), Alamy/F1online digitale Bildagentur GmbH p62(a), Alamy/David Grossman p30(c),
Alamy/Robert Harding World Imagery p42(b), Alamy/Christine Osborne Pictures p50(a),
Alamy/PCN Photography p65(c), Alamy/Prisma Bildagentur AG p46(br), Alamy/Anna Stowe
Landscapes UK p38(b), Alamy/Zuma Press, Inc p78(bcr); **Brand X** pp50(b),62(b); **Corbis**/
Alejandro Almaraz p30(e), Corbis/Ian Taylor/First Light p78(bcl), Corbis/Chris Christodoulou/
Lebrecht Mus/Lebrecht Music & Arts p30(f), Corbis/Ocean p65(d), Corbis/Tomas Rodriguez
p10(b), Corbis/Erik Isakson/Tetra Images p10(a); **Design Pics** p6; **Digital Vision** p62(c);
Getty Images pp30(a),62(d),65(b), Getty Images/Markus Biemüller p38(a), Getty Images/
Mike Clarke p54(c), Getty Images/Comstock Images p22(b), Getty Images/Danita Delimont
p30(d), Getty Images/Tim Graham p58, Getty Images/Blend Images/Hill Street Studios p54(b),
Getty Images/Marta Nardini p17(a), Getty Images/Hans Neleman p65(a), Getty Images/
Dave Porter Peterborough UK p42(d), Getty Images/Westend61 p17(b); **Image Source**
pp14,17(c),42(c); **Photodisc** p48, Photodisc/Getty Images p42(a); **STOCK DISC** p46(bl);
Thinkstock/iStockphoto pp22(a),46(bcm), Thinkstock/Wavebreak Media p81.

Printed and bound in Thailand

2018 2017 2016 2015 2014
10 9 8 7 6 5 4 3 2 1

Contents

Introduction

Are you taking or re-taking your IELTS exam and hoping to gain a high score? Would you like to improve your academic writing skills? If so, this book is designed to help you.

Improve your Skills: Writing for IELTS 6.0–7.5 can be used for self-study or in the classroom with a teacher as part of a course. It can be used alongside other books or studied on its own.

Why use this book?

Successful academic writing is not just about practising a lot, although this helps! It requires you to do a number of things:

- comprehend the process of writing from the first stage (understanding the question) to the final stage (proofreading your final answer)
- recognize and produce the style, features and formats typical of academic writing
- develop the appropriate range of vocabulary, expressions and grammatical forms associated with successful academic writing
- be familiar with typical contexts and topics

Scoring well in the IELTS exam additionally requires you to utilize a variety of exam strategies and techniques, applying the skills and knowledge you have developed to produce a strong answer.

Working systematically through this book should support you in improving all these areas, helping you to understand the requirements of good academic writing then apply them effectively to achieve a higher score in the exam.

The content of the book

Improve your Skills: Writing for IELTS is divided into 10 units. The topics are typical of those found in the exam, ensuring that you have an awareness of likely subject matter.

Each unit is subdivided into three parts: Task 1, Task 2 and a Practice test. There is an answer key at the end of the book, as well as sample answers for the Practice test questions.

Task 1 covers the vocabulary, structures and writing features required to answer the first task in the exam successfully. This means it highlights the necessary language content, including related structures and grammar. It will develop your awareness of the processes of writing to support you in answering Task 1 questions more effectively. It will help you to understand the styles and formats of writing required. Throughout, it will provide practical exercises to give you practice applying this knowledge.

Task 2 repeats the process for the second task in the exam, developing the language, processes and skills needed to tackle this question. Each unit covers different aspects or formats required for Task 2 so that you are familiar with the range of task types which you may meet in the exam.

Technique boxes are found throughout each unit and are designed to give you practical tips and strategies on improving exam performance.

A **Practice test** is found at the end of each unit. Each Practice test gives you an example of both task questions, in the exam format.

Tips for using the book

If studying alone, it is recommended that you work through the book in chronological order as the skills and content build progressively. However, if you are working with a teacher you may be asked to focus on specific areas of the book or you may wish to focus on the content you have most difficulty with.

Using the Practice tests

You can use the Practice tests informally, as extra practice, or as a 'mock' exam, testing yourself either at home or in the class in exam conditions.

Ideally you should do some of the Practice tests in real time, i.e. giving yourself 60 minutes to complete both tasks without using a dictionary or any other support. You may wish to start by splitting the tasks and taking a break between each one. However, it is important to do some of the tests within a set time limit. This will allow you to see how you perform in exam conditions.

Using the Answer key

The key at the end of the book will allow you to check all your answers to the unit exercises. For each of the Practice test questions you will also find sample answers at the back of the book. The sample answers cover a range of student answers, from low to high level, and there is a commentary after each one, highlighting the typical errors and issues in the answer. Some of the high-level samples offer excellent models – though they are not the only way to answer the questions. Other samples are at a lower level and are invaluable in helping you understand the issues and typical errors to be avoided.

Summary of IELTS Writing Test Academic Module requirements

TASK 1	Describing a table, chart, diagram or process using evidence from the graphic provided	20 minutes; minimum 150 words
TASK 2	An essay describing a problem, response or opinion on typical topics	40 minutes; minimum 250 words

Education

UNIT AIMS

TASK 1 Education vocabulary
Identifying and ordering key trends
Overview of visual data questions

TASK 2 Understanding the question
Nouns in questions and introductions
Overview of essay structures

TASK 1 Identifying key information

1 Match the type of education 1–7 with the correct definition a–g. Which type of education are you familiar with?

1	post-graduate	a	learning that includes many areas, e.g. art, sport, social skills
2	continuing	b	learning for older children, usually between ages 11 and 18
3	secondary	c	a course that teaches the skills required for a job
4	higher	d	lessons for adults, often held in the evening, e.g. language lessons
5	well-rounded	e	learning at university or at a similar level, e.g. a degree course
6	vocational	f	basic skills – learning how to read and write properly
7	literacy	g	high-level learning for graduates, e.g. a master's degree/doctorate

2 Read the statements below. Do you agree or disagree with them? Why? Identify at least two reasons in each case.

a Traditional written exams are the most effective way to measure intelligence.
b A successful career is dependent upon going to university.
c Learning a skill through work experience is better than learning it in a classroom.
d Levels of literacy for young people are generally increasing globally.

3 Look at the graph opposite and answer the questions.

a What age group and type of student does the graph show?
b How many countries are included?
c Which years does it cover?

4 On this type of line graph there is always a horizontal axis and a vertical axis. Answer the questions below.

a Which is the Y axis and which is the X axis?
b Put the correct headings 1 or 2 into the gaps a and b on the graph.

1 Year
2 Percentage of 15-year-old children

5 Think about the key trends or patterns you can see in the graph and answer the questions.

   a How many lines show an upward trend overall?
   b How many are downward?
   c Is any line consistently higher and/or consistently lower in general?
   d Can you see any patterns by comparing the start and end points shown?
   e Why has this type of graph been used and not a diagram or pie chart?

6 Look at the exam task below and answer the questions.

   a How much time do you have to complete the task?
   b How many words do you need to write?

> *You should spend about 20 minutes on this task.*
> *[handwritten: population aged 15]*
> **The graph shows the percentage of 15 year olds with low literacy (reading and writing) levels in four countries. Summarize the information by selecting and reporting the main features, and make comparisons where relevant.**
> *[handwritten: SHOWS = Gives information on / provides information on / illustrates information about]*
> *Write at least 150 words.*

> **Technique**
> When writing about graphs, look at the visual information overall without focusing on the details. You will usually be able to identify three or four main trends or patterns. Circle or draw arrows on the graph to highlight the key features and patterns. Consider: upward and downward movements, highest and lowest points and the start and end points for the range of information shown. Identifying key trends will help you structure your writing.

7 Read the model text below. Match paragraphs a–d with summaries 1–4.

   1 Gives an overview ___D___

   2 Describes main upward trends ___C___

   3 Describes the main downward trend ___B___

   4 Introduction describing data set ___A___

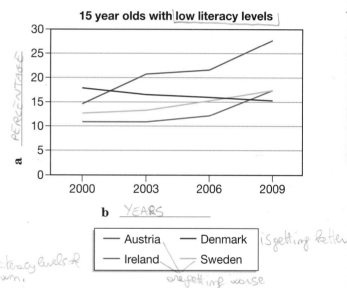

15 year olds with low literacy levels

[y-axis: PERCENTAGE (a)]
[x-axis: YEARS (b)] — 2000, 2003, 2006, 2009

Legend: — Austria — Denmark *[handwritten: is getting better]* — Ireland — Sweden *[handwritten: are getting worse]*

   a The graph provides information about the literacy rates of 15 year olds in four European countries over a period of nine years.

   b There are two clear trends visible. Only one country, Denmark, experienced a slight fall in poor literacy levels, as numbers dropped marginally from around 17 per cent in 2000 to 15 per cent in 2009. This minor dip nevertheless gave Denmark the lowest percentage overall by the end of the period shown. *[handwritten: meaning Denmark has the best literacy levels of the 4 country shown.]*

   c Conversely, in the majority of countries the proportion of children with low literacy levels increased, the biggest rise being evident in Austria. This country had the highest number of children with weak literacy throughout the period, except in the year 2000 where, at 15 per cent, the numbers were approximately 2 per cent lower than those in Denmark. However, by 2003 Austrian numbers had reached just over 20 per cent and rose again more steeply to a high of around 27 per cent in 2009. Ireland and Sweden both saw steady upward trends in their totals, beginning with around 11 per cent and 13 per cent respectively and ending at a similar percentage of 17 per cent.

   d Therefore, with the exception of Denmark, the percentage of 15 year olds with literacy problems generally went up. The difference between the countries was relatively low in 2000, ranging from around 11 per cent to 17 per cent, but this difference grew and by 2009 spanned from approximately 15 per cent to over 27 per cent.

[handwritten notes:]
① In Denmark the level of literacy is actually rising.
② In 2000 Den. had worst literacy levels, but by 2009 had best.
③ Ireland/Sweden similar trend end same point
④

Unit 1

Guided model

8 Look at the graph. Quickly check the title and axis to find out:

  a what the chart shows.

  b what the numbers refer to.

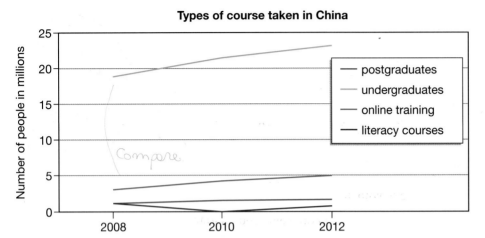

Types of course taken in China

Legend:
— postgraduates
— undergraduates
— online training
— literacy courses

Y-axis: Number of people in millions (0–25)
X-axis: 2008, 2010, 2012

Compare

9 Identify three to four key trends in the graph. Use the questions below to help you.

  a How many of the lines show an upward trend? How many show a downward trend?

  b Which line is consistently higher? Which is consistently lower?

  c What are the similarities and differences between the start and end points?

10 Look at the summary table below. Complete the table with notes about the graph.

1 Introduction	*Data identified – 4 types of course in China* *Dates specified – 2008-2012*
2 Downward trends	
3 Upward trends	
4 Overview	*Final summary*

> ## Technique
>
> You need to identify key trends and patterns in the data, and use details to support this information. If you list a lot of information about each part of the graph separately, you will not be demonstrating an ability to select and group information effectively. If you do not include supporting details, you will lose marks. Spend two or three minutes identifying key trends and use this to structure your answer. Add supporting details after identifying the main features.

11 Read the example question and model answer below. Ignore the gaps. Number the paragraphs a–d in the correct order. Does the model answer contain similar information to your notes?

> *The graph shows the number of students enrolled on different course types in China. Summarize the information by selecting and reporting the main information.*
>
> *Write at least 150 words.*

2 **a** The first key feature shows that literacy courses had the lowest number of participants overall for the whole period. This type of course is the only one which showed a ~~downward trend~~, beginning with just over 1.5 million students in 2008 then ~~dipping to~~ almost 0 by 2010. Uptake ~~rose~~ slightly in 2012 to just under a million but this course type remained the lowest in terms of student numbers.

4 **b** Overall, with the exception of literacy, the number of students on all the other courses climbed ~~gradually~~ with undergraduates easily outnumbering all other types of student.

1 **c** The graph ~~demonstrates~~ the number of people enrolled on four different types of educational course in China in the period 2008 to 2012.

3 **d** On the other hand, the proportion of students on undergraduate courses showed the highest increase throughout the period and numbers on this type of course ~~increased steadily~~ from around 19 million in 2008 to 23 million in 2012. These courses had approximately four times as many students as the other types of course. Similarly, numbers of students enrolled as postgraduates and using online courses followed a similar ~~upward trend~~ and increased moderately from 2008 to 2012, ending with around 2 million and 5 million participants respectively in 2012.

a Pie chart

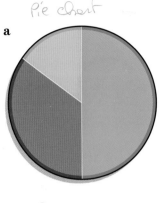

b table

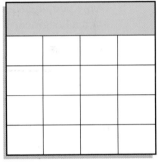

c bar chart

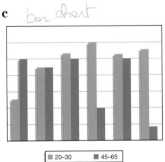

20–30   45–65

12 Read the model answer again in the correct order. Complete the answer with words from the box.

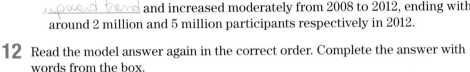

> demonstrates ▪ dipping to ▪ downward trend ▪ gradually ▪ increased steadily
> rose ▪ upward trend

13 Match the visuals a–d with correct names from the box.

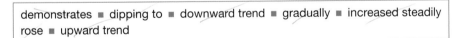

> bar chart ▪ pie chart ▪ process diagram ▪ table

14 Look at the visuals in 13 again and answer the questions.
   a Which two visual figures can also show trends? C
   b Which of the visuals is best for high levels of detail? B
   c Which visual helps highlight proportions or parts within a whole data set? A
   d Which visual helps highlight comparisons between different categories of a data set? C

d Process diagram

plans → researching → drawing → making → servicing

Technique

Line graphs are useful for showing overall trends. There are four other types of visual you might write about in Task 1: bar chart, pie chart, process diagram, table.

Task 2 Understanding the question

1 Look at the pictures. What kinds of issues do they show in relation to education today?

2 Answer the questions, giving reasons in each case.

a What do you think about technology in education? What are the pros and cons?

b Some people believe more women should be encouraged to study subjects such as engineering. Do you agree or disagree? Why?

c Why do you think some children dislike school and leave as early as possible? How could this problem be reduced?

d What are the advantages and disadvantages of going to university? Do you think it is a good idea overall?

Technique

In Task 2 of the exam you will answer an essay question. There are usually four types of question. Understanding the type can help you plan and answer the question more effectively.

3 Match each type of essay 1–4 with a definition and sample question a–d.

1 Theory-based essay	**a discuss different views and reach your own conclusion** *Students are relying more and more upon technology and the internet to study. Some people see this as a <u>benefit</u>; others believe students are losing their ability to think for themselves.* *Discuss both points of view and give your own opinion.*
2 Contrasting viewpoints essay	**b suggest solutions or evaluate solutions to a problem** *Some young people find school difficult and leave early without any qualifications. What causes this problem and what <u>measures</u> could help reduce it?*
3 Evaluation and opinion essay	**c evaluate a statement and justify your own <u>opinion</u> on the topic (you may or may not include opposing viewpoints)** *University education should only be offered to the most academic students, not a large majority. To what extent do you agree?*
4 Problem-solving essay	**d present your own ideas about an issue, discussing possible <u>causes</u> and effects** *Many more men than women choose to study maths and engineering. Why is this? Gives reasons for your answers and include any relevant examples from your own knowledge or experience.*

Technique

Look carefully at the essay question for key words. Examples of these are underlined in the table in 3. Ensure that you analyse the question fully before you begin to plan. Use the key words to help you in two ways: to identify the question type and to help you include all the necessary sections in your answer.

4 The box below contains key words from 3. Complete the table by putting nouns from the box in the correct category. The words may be synonyms, antonyms or related words.

advantage ■ attitude ■ channels ■ difficulty ■ disagreement ■ drawback ■ effect ■ hindrance methods ■ opposition ■ point of view ■ procedures ■ reasons ■ roots ■ sources ■ steps

Measures	Opinion	Benefit	Causes
		advantage	

5 Match the word categories in 4 to the essay types in 3. There may be more than one possible answer.

For a theory-based essay I will probably see the language of causes.

6 Complete the introductions for essays a–d in 3. Use the correct form of words from the table in 4. There may be more than one possible answer.

> **Technique**
> All the nouns in 4 are commonly found in Task 2 questions. Knowing these will help you identify what is being asked.

a Whilst it is unarguable that technology has provided many _____ to students, helping them with their studies, it is also possible that there are _____ which impact negatively on their ability to use their own initiative and mental facilities.

b There are many _____ why some children leave full-time education too
ᴄ early to benefit them; it is therefore important to take _____ to prevent this damaging behaviour.

c There is no doubt that people have differing _____ about who should have access to university education. According to many, it is important that the most able students go.

d Men tend to outnumber women in maths and engineering courses for a number of _____ . These vary from social expectations to personal preference but the _____ is the same: fewer females choose particular subjects to study.

7 Read the task below and answer the questions.
a How many words do you need to write?
b How long do you have to do this?
c Why is it not a good idea to extend the time or number of words?
d Which essay type is this: theory, contrasting viewpoints, evaluation and opinion or problem-solving? Which phrase tells you?
e Underline the statement in the first part of the question. What are the two key elements you need to agree or disagree about?

> *You should spend about 40 minutes on this task.*
> **Some people believe that university education should only be offered to those who can pay for their own courses and the government should not be expected to fund higher education. To what extent do you agree?**
> *Write at least 250 words.*

8 Read the model answer below. Label the sections of the essay a–e with phrases from the box.

> introducing topic ■ justifying opinion (x2) ■ stating opinion ■ summarizing point of view

In a number of countries, those at university have their degree courses funded by the government but many people nowadays assert that students should pay themselves. Whilst there are many reasons to justify such a viewpoint, I don't entirely agree with it.

a ....

¹ ...., the benefits of having a well-educated population are felt by all those in society. This is because the general population gains when there is a ready supply of good doctors, engineers, teachers and businesspeople who can contribute to the welfare of all. Therefore it seems fair that all members of society should contribute through a tax system in order to pay for such education.

b ....

² ...., it is important that those who train to undertake such roles are the most able and competent in the country. Should education be too expensive, it is likely that some of the most capable and talented young people may be discouraged from studying, especially if they happen to come from a poorer background. Indeed, if the tax system is organized so that those earning more pay a higher level of tax, then probably most graduates will pay back a good deal into society over many years of work. Their education will help them get better employment so they will probably contribute more money over a lifetime.

c ....

It is ³ .... important to remember that an educated and cultured society is a civilized one and, in principle, I believe that education should be available to all young people and that their financial background should not hold them back.

d ....

⁴ ...., while some people argue that government money should not be spent on the university education of individuals, I disagree entirely. I feel that society as a whole benefits from supporting students in higher education so the government should fund these costs.

e ....

9 Complete the model answer with organizing phrases from the box.

> also ■ firstly ■ furthermore ■ in conclusion

Technique

Keep your introduction brief and don't copy out the rubric (question). Ensure each paragraph has a clear topic and there is a final conclusion. If you are writing an opinion or 'contrasting viewpoints' essay, make sure your position is clearly presented.

Practice Test 1

Task 1

You should spend about 20 minutes on this task.

The graph shows the amount earned by graduates of different age groups in 2002. It includes those with a degree, those with a higher degree (postgraduate) and those with other qualifications. Summarize the information by selecting and reporting the main features, and make comparisons where relevant.

Write at least 150 words.

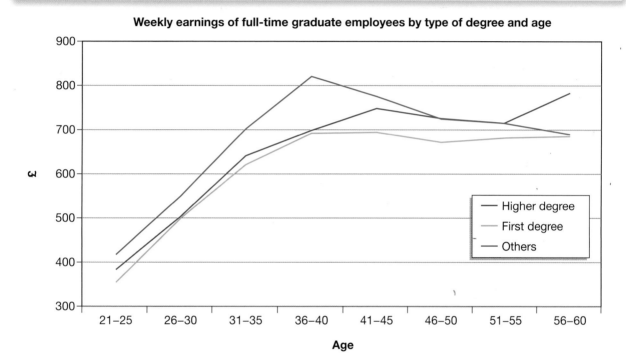

Weekly earnings of full-time graduate employees by type of degree and age

Task 2

You should spend about 40 minutes on this task.

Some people suggest that children do not understand the world of work and schools should make all teenagers spend a short time working as well as studying academic subjects. To what extent do you agree?

Write at least 250 words.

2

Communication
and the internet

UNIT AIMS

TASK 1　Noun phrases
　　　　Describing trends
　　　　Adjectives and adverbs

TASK 2　Adjective and noun forms to
　　　　establish opinion
　　　　Introducing an evaluation and
　　　　opinion essay
　　　　Organizing ideas

Task 1 Noun phrases

1 Complete the diagram with collocations. Use words from the box.

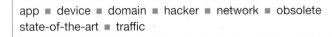

> app ■ device ■ domain ■ hacker ■ network ■ obsolete
> state-of-the-art ■ traffic

7 ....

8 ....

6 ....

technology

1 ...... *network* ......

mobile

computer

5 ....

2 ....

internet

4 ....

3 ....

2 Choose two phrases from the diagram. Think of three ways that these things affect your own life.

At work I keep all my documents on a computer network because different staff members have to access them. When the network goes down it is annoying because I can't do any work. I don't have a computer network at home unless you count the internet.

Technique

Look out for nouns with the same or similar meaning in adjacent sentences. You may be able to combine them into one sentence, e.g. the nouns *brand* and *device* are used in a similar way in the example below so can be combined easily.

3 The sentences in a have been rewritten as a single sentence. Following the same pattern, rewrite sentences b–f.

a The first mobile phone was a Motorola brand. It was a 9-inch device and an important innovation.
   The first mobile phone, a 9-inch Motorola device, was an important innovation.

b Mobile apps are software applications. They are downloadable tools and are often free.

c The cloud is a virtual space on the internet. It is a storage environment not reliant on a PC.

d The first website went online in 1991. It was a French-based technical web page.

e Instant messaging allows quick transmission of text. It is an enhanced mode of communication in real time.

f Smart phones have a wide variety of applications. They are one of the biggest selling technological devices available.

Technique

Use a variety of vocabulary and grammar forms in order to make your writing interesting. Repeating words and structures makes a text dull and difficult to read.

(handwritten: ✶ Turkey steady increase ✶ Poland steady decrease)

4 Look at the Task 1 question below. What key trends can you see in the table?

> *The table gives information about the number of people working as researchers in technology per million people in five countries. Summarize the information by selecting and reporting the main features, and make comparisons where relevant.*

(handwritten left margin: Comparison ✶)

	2003	2004	2005	2006	2007
Turkey	47	50	70	83	106
Poland	285	263	234	227	226
Mexico	147	212	242	179	183
Moldova	103	92	89	97	114
Togo	18	17	23	17	18

(handwritten right annotations: Double the amount / Highest / Decrease / increased / fluctuation / be erratic / Lowest)

5 Read the sentences about the table. Look at the words in italics. Which is NOT correct?

1 The table *illustrates/provides data about/draws* the number of technology researchers per million of population who were working in five countries from 2003 to 2007.

2 Mexico and Togo followed a similar *pattern/style/trend* as they both reached a peak in 2005, with 242 and 23 researchers *respectively/in turn/each*.

3 The number of researchers in Mexico was greater than for Togo *in general/overall/in summary*.

4 In Turkey numbers *climbed/slipped/increased* steadily from 47 in 2003 to over double that in 2007.

5 Poland's numbers *fell/peaked/dipped* to 226 in 2007 although they remained higher than those of any other country for most of the period.

6 The last two sentences in 5 describe upward and downward movements in the data. Write the verbs from the two sentences in the correct place in the table below.

Verbs showing downward movement	Verbs showing upward movement	Verbs showing little or no movement
Decline *Decrease* *Drop* *Go down* *Plunge* *Slump*	*climbed,* *Go up* *Grow (to)* *Reach* *Rise* *Soar*	*Hold (steady at)* *Level (off)* *Remain (stable at)* *Stay (constant at)* *Range* *Span*

7 Add the verbs below to the correct place in the table in 6.

> decline ■ decrease ■ drop ■ go down ■ go up ■ grow (to) ■ hold (steady at) ■ level (off)
> plunge ■ range ■ reach ■ remain (stable at) ■ rise ■ slump ■ soar ■ span ■ stay (constant at)

(handwritten: oscillare (from the lowest to the highest numb.)   crollo   estendersi (distanza) (time period))

8 Match 1–3 with a–c to make sentences about Mexico. Underline the adverb in each sentence.

1 The number of researchers in Mexico   a rose very slightly, ending at a total of 183.

2 From 2005 to 2006 numbers   b increased dramatically to a high of 242.

3 Finally they   c dropped steeply again to 179.

1 C
2 D
3 B

9 Look at the line graphs opposite. Which line a–d matches sentence 1 about Mexico in 8? Which matches sentences 2 and 3?

1

10 Match the sentences a–d to the line graphs opposite. Then write the adverbs in the correct place in the table below.

> dramatically ■ gradually ■ marginally ■ markedly ■ moderately ■ modestly
> noticeably ■ progressively ■ sharply ■ significantly ■ slightly ■ steadily

a The numbers rose. b The numbers dropped.	c The numbers soared. d The numbers plunged.
1	7 _dramatically_
2	8
3	9
4	10
5	11
6	12

2

11 Draw two lines below to match the adverbs in bold in a and b.

   a The numbers fluctuated **wildly**.   **b** The numbers varied **gently**.

12 Read the sentences below. Which sentence has the pattern verb + adverb and which has the pattern *there is/was* + adjective + noun?

   a The number of researchers in Mexico rose dramatically to a high of 242.
   b There was a dramatic rise in the number of researchers to a high of 242.

13 Rewrite the sentences below using the alternative pattern.

   a In Turkey numbers increased steadily from 47 in 2003 to over double that in 2007.

   b There was a slight fall in Poland's numbers to 226 in 2007.

   c From 2005 to 2006 we can see a steep drop in Mexican numbers to 179.

   d Finally they rose very slightly, ending at a total of 183.

14 Look at the information about Moldova in 4. Write one sentence about the data using the pattern verb + adverb and one sentence using the pattern *there is/was* + adjective + noun.

> **Technique**
>
> Include adverbs or adverbial phrases in Task 1 answers in order to show that you can evaluate the data given. Make sure that the adverb you choose collocates (matches) with an appropriate verb, e.g. *The numbers soared modestly dramatically*.

> **Technique**
>
> If you find it difficult to work with the numbers in a table, draw a very rough line graph of the information first to help you visualize it. Alternatively put a small 'up' ↗ 'down' ↘ or 'level' → arrow after each number in the table comparing it to the preceding number, to help you see the trend.

Task 2 Giving opinions

1 What current issues related to the use of the internet and mobile technology does each picture show?

2 Make a list of the pros and cons of the internet and related technology. Think about

a communication.
b study.
c socializing.
d work.

3 Read the statements below. Do you agree or disagree with them? Why?

1 Undoubtedly, mobile devices are popular because they are so convenient.
2 Obviously, the rise in illegal downloads is due to the proliferation of websites which make this possible.
3 Inevitably, people are increasingly reliant on technology to complete everyday activities.
4 Naturally, social networking has led to an increase in online bullying.
5 Shockingly, there is an unhealthy rise in the number of children under 10 who have access to online technology without supervision.
6 Sadly, bookshops have been affected by the rise of online publications, reducing the number of books being sold on the high street.
7 Interestingly, the advent of text messaging is encouraging an increase in the amount that young people write, even though this may not be extensive.
8 Realistically, a computerized society leads to a society in which people are less, not more, connected to each other.

4 Does the writer agree with the statements in 3? Underline the word in each statement that shows the writer's opinion.

5 Look at the groups of adverbs/adverbial phrases below. If you replace the adverbs in 3 with those in each group below, how does this change the attitude shown by the writer?

Group 1: generally speaking/by and large/typically

Group 2: unfortunately/disturbingly/worryingly

Group 3: importantly/significantly/notably

Group 4: probably/apparently/as might be expected

a

b

c

6 Choose the best answer (A, B, C or D) for each space.

1 Evidence has _____ shown that too much gaming can damage children's concentration.

2 _____ , a higher level of funding in technological research will lead to better results and new technological developments some years later.

3 _____ , younger people are more likely to be 'digital natives' and older people tend to be 'digital immigrants'.

4 _____ , 70 per cent of teenagers report seeing cyberbullying on a regular basis.

1 **A** highly   **B** clearly   **C** strongly   **D** vastly
2 **A** Unfortunately   **B** Conclusively   **C** Without doubt   **D** Severely
3 **A** Apparently   **B** Seriously   **C** Distinctly   **D** Worryingly
4 **A** Consistently   **B** Probably   **C** Amazingly   **D** Disturbingly

7 Complete each sentence with an adverb to suggest the opinion shown in brackets. There may be more than one possible answer.

1   **a** _____ , older people are not good with technology.   (This is generally true.)
    b _____ , (This is inevitable.)
    c _____ , (This is a bad thing.)

2   **a** _____ , people spend a lot of their time online.   (Everyone knows this.)
    b _____ , (This could be a problem.)
    c _____ , (This has a key impact.)

3   **a** _____ , multinational companies have too much control over what appears on the internet.   (This is terrible.)
    b _____ , (This is definitely true.)
    b _____ , (This is mostly true.)

> **Technique**
> When writing an evaluation and opinion essay or a viewpoints essay, use adverbs and adverbial phrases to identify the position you are taking.

8 Read the Task 2 question below and decide which kind of essay it is.

   a theory-based essay
   b contrasting viewpoints essay
   c evaluation and opinion essay
   d problem-solving essay

> *Some people suggest that social networking and online communication have increased social isolation. In what ways do you think this has happened? Give reasons for your answers and include any relevant examples from your own knowledge or experience.*
> *Write at least 250 words.*

WHY?

Addicted to internet

everybody bec SP
PPl always online
New technologies are attractive
easier to spend time with fec.
do most things online

9 Complete the notes below with ideas for the Task 2 question in 8.

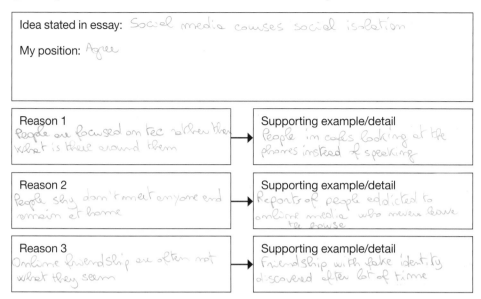

Idea stated in essay: Social media causes social isolation

My position: Agree

Reason 1
People are focused on tec rather than what is there around them
→ Supporting example/detail
People in cafes looking at the phones instead of speaking

Reason 2
People shy don't meet anyone and remain at home
→ Supporting example/detail
Reports of people addicted to online media who never leave the house

Reason 3
Online friendship are often not what they seem
→ Supporting example/detail
Friendship with fake identity discovered after lot of time

10 Read the model answer below. Do you think the writer had similar notes to you or were the points different?

In recent years the use of social networking has grown beyond recognition, bringing a new set of concerns with it. 20 Most young people now text regularly and are familiar with a variety of other platforms used for communication, such as FaceTime and instant messaging. It has never been easier to keep in touch with family and friends wherever they are in the world. Despite this, however, there is evidence that social isolation is rising and not decreasing. I therefore agree that rather than helping people communicate, technology has actually weakened social bonds. I will attempt to outline some key reasons for this. 81

1 Firstly and most obviously, if people are using tablets, phones or other devices, they are focused on the technology rather than what is happening around them. While this might help us keep in touch with people who are far away from us (for example those travelling), often it means that the user forgets those in their vicinity. For example, it is now common to see people in restaurants and cafes all looking at their phones instead of speaking to each other. 81

2 Secondly, although using social networks might seem a good solution for someone who is shy or worried about meeting others, ironically it is more likely to keep them at home. In fact, if people didn't have that option they would have to go out and meet real friends, which is a much healthier way to deal with being lonely. There are reports of people who rarely leave their houses because they are addicted to an 'online existence' and young people who become aggressive when their parents tell them to come offline. 90

3 Finally, even if people do meet online friends, these friendships are often not really what they seem. Unfortunately, there have been several reports of people being harmed by someone they believed was a friend. This is because the internet allows us to disguise who we really are. As honesty is key to a good relationship, clearly this is not a good basis to meet friends. 66

In conclusion, I would argue that while the internet can help with quick and convenient communication for business or travel, or when people live in distant places, for a number of reasons it has not increased social cohesion overall. 39

377

11 Underline the adverbs and other phrases in 10 that show the opinion of the writer.

Technique

Reading news articles and noticing the language used will improve your own writing and ensure you have some ideas for some of the typical topics that appear in the exam.

Unit 2

12 Below is a description of the elements in the introductory paragraph in 10. Read the paragraph again and number each item in the order they appear in the text.

5 **a** explain the structure of the essay
4 **b** clarify if the writer agrees or disagrees with the viewpoint given
3 **c** state an assertion or viewpoint (often taken from the question)
1 **d** introduce the essay topic
2 **e** give some background context/examples of the topic

13 Match the phrases 1–12 with the elements a–e in 12.

1 I shall argue that ..B.
2 The main aim of the essay is A. D
3 Initially I will A. before going on to A.
4 It seems to me that B.
5 One commonly held idea is C.
6 I would maintain/suggest that B
7 In recent years it is clear D. E
8 A typical argument is that C.
9 This essay explores the issue of D...
10 Reports often suggest that E. C
11 This issue has become more important as E..
12 This essay will firstly A. then A.

14 Look at the Task 2 question below. Number the sentences a–d in a logical order to make an introductory paragraph.

> ***The internet is often harmful, especially to young people, due to the amount***
> ***and type of information people can access. To what extent do you agree?***
> *Give reasons for your answer and include any relevant examples from*
> *your own experience.*

2 **a** However, it has also never been easier for young people to access information that is not appropriate, such as violent or adult sites.
1 **b** Nowadays most houses have at least one computer or a mobile device so young people and children have constant access to the internet. This can be a useful tool for their school work and for keeping in touch with friends.
3 **c** While there is no doubt this can be a drawback to the benefits of the internet, it seems to me that the problem could be reduced with greater control over the access of young people to the internet; the internet itself is not particularly harmful.
4 **d** This essay explores several reasons why the internet could be considered a positive rather than a harmful factor in people's lives.

15 Match each key point 1–3 with the correct supporting details a–c.

Key points
1 Most information on the internet – useful and informative.
2 Some inappropriate information available – parents should control this.
3 Important for young people to learn how to select information.

Supporting details
a Key life skill – knowing how to see what is true and what is misleading, e.g. conspiracy theories typical but young people should learn how to weigh up evidence.
b Internet helps young people with research skills and very helpful learning tool for school or university and outside.
c Always likely to be inappropriate information, e.g. violent or adult sites, but there are filters and controls that parents can use to control access to these.

Technique

When you plan, note down your key points. Then use a different coloured pencil or pen and add a note of a possible example or detail so that each point has supporting information.

Practice Test 2

Task 1

You should spend about 20 minutes on this task.

The table shows the number of mobile phones sold in millions for a period of six years. Summarize the information by selecting and reporting the main features, and make comparisons where relevant.

Write at least 150 words.

	Nokia	Ericsson	Samsung	Motorola	Apple
2006	345	74	117	210	
2007	436	102	154	165	2.3
2008	475	95	202	108	12
2009	442	57	238	59	24
2010	463	42	282	39	42
2011	422	33	330	40	89
2012	335	28	396.5	28	135.8

Task 2

You should spend about 40 minutes on this task.

To what extent has the internet made life more convenient? Give reasons for your answer and include any relevant examples from your own knowledge or experience.

Write at least 250 words.

3 Tourism and travel

UNIT AIMS

TASK 1   Travel and tourism vocabulary
         Describing a flow chart
         Cause and consequence

TASK 2   Noun phrases
         Structuring viewpoints
         Presenting and refuting a viewpoint

Task 1 Cause and consequence

1 Write the words in the correct place in the table below.

> attraction ■ backpacking trip ■ baggage reclaim ■ cruise ■ domestic visitor
> guide ■ harbour ■ have itchy feet ■ have the travel bug ■ heritage site
> package tour ■ passenger ■ resort ■ tourist ■ trip ■ untouched destinations
> voyage ■ weekend break

Places	People and characteristics	Types of journey/holiday

Technique

Try to develop your knowledge of vocabulary related to current affairs and topics typically found in the exam. Record new words in lexical groups, e.g. words related to travel and tourism.

2 Which types of journey do you prefer and why? How do you prefer to travel? Which places do you enjoy?

3 Which of the places in the pictures would you prefer to visit? Why?

a

b

4 The pictures in 3 are both of Cancun. Read the information below and complete sentences a–c using information from the text.

 **MEXICO TRAVEL**

A remote fishing village until recently, Cancun in Mexico is now a major centre for tourism. This previously untouched destination was identified as a potentially popular resort in 1967 *as a result of* its beautiful coastline, vicinity to important heritage sites and hours of sunshine. The prediction turned out to be correct. Since then, the little village has been transformed into a contemporary city with good electricity and water supplies, conference centres and attractions such as golf courses. It is now one of the most successful new resorts in the world and is visited by 4 million people each year. In part its success is *due to* the growth of low-cost airlines and *because of* huge investment.

   a Someone in 1967 identified Cancun as _____ .

   b Developers have transformed it into a _____ .

   c Four million people _____ .

> **Technique**
>
> Use a range of structures to keep your writing varied. Don't write everything in the same tense or voice as it will not be interesting to read.

5 Compare the sentences in the text which have a similar meaning to the sentences a–c in 4.

   a What do you notice about the form in the text compared to the form in sentences a–c?

   b Why is the form *be* + past participle used?

6 Complete the sentences using the text.

   a Its beautiful beaches, the weather and the cultural sites *meant that* it

_____ .

   b Low-cost airlines grew and *as a consequence* Cancun

_____ .

   c Huge investment was also made in the city and *for this reason*

_____ .

7 Look at the words in *italics* in the text in 4 and in sentences a–c in 6. Write them in the correct place in the table, making any changes necessary.

Cause	Consequence/Effect	
As a consequence of **1** _____ **2** _____ **3** _____	large numbers of tourists, pollution and congestion can increase.	
Large numbers of tourists go to popular resorts	. *Therefore,* . *Consequently,* and **4** _____ which **5** _____ and **6** _____	prices rise.

8 The diagram shows what happens when a tourist arrives at a US airport. Number the sentences a–g in the correct order to describe the process.

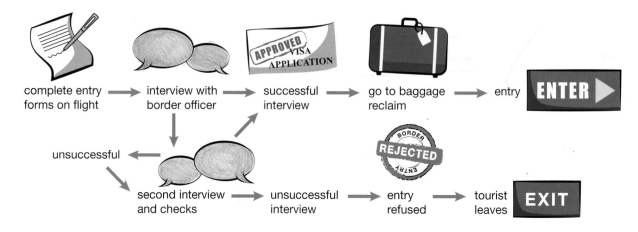

complete entry forms on flight → interview with border officer → successful interview → go to baggage reclaim → entry **ENTER**

unsuccessful ←

second interview and checks → unsuccessful interview → entry refused → tourist leaves **EXIT**

APPROVED VISA APPLICATION

REJECTED BORDER ENTRY

7 **a** In this final phase, the second interview may resolve any problems and for this reason the tourist will be approved for entry. However if the second interview is still a problem, the tourist may have to leave due to the negative outcome. *7*

2 **b** First of all the tourist completes an entry form during the flight and ___gets___ (get) his/her passport and visa ready. *2*

4 **c** If approved, the tourist then ___goes___ (go) to baggage reclaim to collect his/her luggage and can enter the country. *4*

1 **d** The process shown in the diagram illustrates the steps followed when a tourist goes through the immigration process to enter the USA. *1*

e The next stage is at the airport. On arrival, the form ___is inspected___ (inspect) by a border officer and the tourist is asked questions. A decision ___is made___ (made) as *3* a consequence of this interview. *3*

5 **f** This decision is the end of the process for most people because there is no complication and therefore entry is approved. *5*

6 **g** Occasionally there are some concerns in the interview and because of this, a second interview may be required. *6*

9 Complete the sentences in 8 with the active or passive form of the verbs in brackets.

10 Underline the phrases in the sentences in 8 that show cause and effect.

11 Read the sentences in 8 again. Circle the signposting language which helped you put the sentences in the correct order. Add them to the table below.

Opening stages	*firstly,*
Middle stages	*in the next phase,*
Final stages	*finally,*

12 Write the words from the box in the correct place in the table.

after this ■ at the end ■ in the first stage
in the last stage ■ next ■ subsequently

Technique

When writing about a process it is important to be clear about the order of events. Use signposting language for clarity.

13 Look at the Task 2 question and diagram below. Use the sentence stems a–h to write sentences about the diagram. Use the cause and effect phrases in 10 and the signposting language from the table in 11.

> *You should spend about 20 minutes on this task.*
>
> **The diagram shows the process in which a tourist resort can develop and grow. Summarize the information by selecting and reporting the main features.**
>
> *Write at least 150 words.*

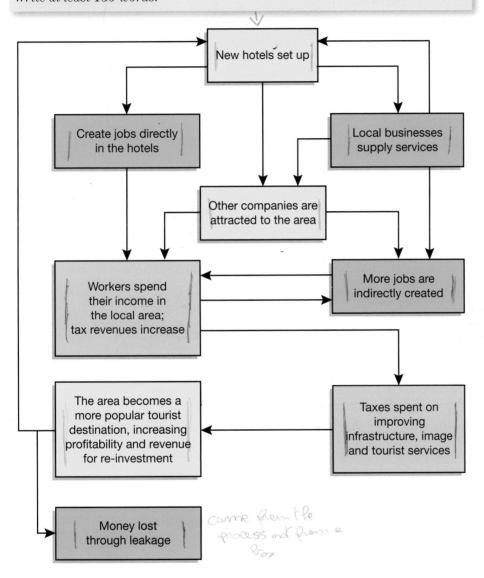

Money lost through leakage — *come from the process not from a box* (handwritten)

a diagram/illustrates/small resort/change to larger one
b new hotels/set up
c create/jobs/hotels
d local businesses/supply hotels/create more jobs
e workers/at hotel and in local business/spend money locally/generate more tax and income for local area
f tax income/improved infrastructure, image, tourist services
g more popular/more profits and revenue for reinvestment
h new hotels built

Technique

If you are writing about a process, you can talk about cause and effect if these are clear from the flow chart or diagram. However, if you are writing about statistical trends, e.g. a bar chart or line graph, don't make suppositions about the reasons for what you are describing.

Unit 3

Task 2 **Noun phrases**

1 Read the information about tourism. Which area of the world is the most popular with tourists? Why is tourism important?

> Europe is the biggest 'tourist resort' in the world, taking 25 per cent of [1] money spent around the globe on tourism. [2] Tourism boards have recently released figures which show that within Europe, four countries are the [3] destinations that most people choose: of all the visitors, over half go to France, Spain, Italy or the UK. Eighty per cent of all [4] tourists who are over 18 include a cultural activity on their holiday such as a visit to a [5] place with cultural or historical interest. So any [6] finances that are drained for the upkeep of such tourist attractions is covered by income from their visits, along with [7] the other things tourists spend money on. This is important as there is a correlation between tourism and the future [8] way the economy develops in that country.

2 Match the underlined phrases in the text in 1 with one of the noun phrases a–h.
  - **a** development of the economy
  - **b** other expenditure
  - **c** global spend
  - **d** the release of recent figures
  - **e** destinations of choice
  - **f** adult tourists
  - **g** heritage site
  - **h** drain on finances

3 Match a–h in 2 with the noun patterns below. Some can fit more than one category.

  - **a** noun 'of' noun _____

  - **b** noun in object position _____

  - **c** compound noun _____

  - **d** noun phrase with preposition _____

4 Which improves the flow of the paragraph, the original phrase or the replacement?

5 Rewrite the sentences below using one of the noun patterns in 3 and the word in brackets.

  1 The number of tourists coming to a host country is a key factor in improving its economy. (tourism)

   Levels _____ economy _____ the host country.

  2 The tour guide was particularly bad because she was not capable of organizing the group. (capacity)

   The tour guide was particularly bad because she had _____ the group.

  3 Resorts with beaches are popular for relaxing holidays. (beach)

   _____ are popular for relaxing holidays.

  4 Some local communities begin to rely on the income earned through tourism. (reliant upon)

   Some _____ income.

Technique

We use noun forms to improve ~~the way that we write things~~ *our writing style* and reduce ~~the amount of space needed to describe things~~ *the economy of our writing*.

6 Look at the Task 2 question below and underline the key words. Does the question ask you to think about more than one opinion?

> *You should spend about 40 minutes on this task.*
> *superene*
> **Some people believe the benefits of <u>tourism outweigh the problems it</u>**
> **<u>creates in a particular place</u>. Discuss both views and give your own**
> **opinion.**
> *Write at least 250 words.*

Contrasting view point

Tourism in a perticular place

7 Brainstorm a list of benefits and disadvantages related to tourism and make some notes. For each benefit, try to think of any disadvantages, and vice versa.

Benefits	Disadvantages
- Place become famous - More money to the place - More investors *support/exemple* - Develop of transport	- Too many people means traffic jam - Everything become expensive also for the citizien - Place completely transformed/Lost of identity

8 Look at the model plan below. Were your ideas similar?

Introduction: growth of tourism seen as benefit (resorts bring in money and other advantages). But some people complain about negative effect (environmental damage/increasing prices). Will look at the different aspects of tourism; argue that it can be both beneficial and cause problems.

Technique

When writing essays, a common mistake students make is not planning enough. Spend a few minutes brainstorming ideas, e.g. using a benefits/ disadvantages table or a mind map, before writing. You can then focus on language issues.

Idea one:
for

against

Benefit: brings in money/local economy improves – more jobs for local people
Disadvantage: also increases costs, e.g. house prices go up and prices aimed at tourists so local people suffer; jobs only seasonal

Idea two:
for

against

Benefit: tourism improves infrastructure – more facilities for tourists/transportation better, etc. – helps local population, too
Disadvantages: damages the environment/not good long term, e.g. beautiful area gets overdeveloped

Idea three:
for

against

Benefit: brings in new people/new types of attractions and cafes, etc.
Disadvantages: history and culture sometimes damaged – becomes very commercialized

You are super beautiful this morning!

Conclusion: benefits of tourism very clear – commercially good for an area. Key point – must be done with care or becomes damaging. Therefore I believe tourism largely beneficial but only if done with controls.

9 Read the model paragraph for 'Idea one'. Underline the sentence that introduces a benefit and the sentence that introduces a contrasting disadvantage.

> At first glance, tourism seems to be a huge advantage for the local area. Certainly, it can bring in a lot of money and the growth in hotels and the service industry ensures that the local economy improves rapidly. In addition to this, job creation means that more of the people living in the area can find work. Nevertheless, the assumption that tourism is always a benefit is increasingly under fire. Incoming money pushes up prices so, although the local economy improves, house prices and costs for local people increase as well. The improvement in employment levels can help but even this is not all positive; much of the work created is seasonal, meaning people are still unemployed for part of the year.

10 Decide which of the sentences introduce an argument (a) and which introduce an opposing idea (b). Write (a) or (b) next to each sentence.

1 It is often assumed that A
2 Although I have some sympathy for this view, it is also true that B.
3 The view that A. is gaining popularity.
4 A commonly held view is that A.
5 However, this makes the assumption that B.
6 It seems a fair suggestion that A.
7 An argument that is often asserted is A
8 Although there is some truth to these ideas, it is also true to say B.

11 Match the verb phrases 1–6 with an equivalent noun phrase a–f.

1 It is often assumed that …B   **a** Although accurate in part, these ideas …
2 Although I sympathize with this view E.   **b** However, this makes the assumption that …
3 A commonly held view is that .D   **c** It seems a fair suggestion (that) …
4 It seems reasonable to suggest (that) C.   **d** A common view is that …
5 An argument that is often asserted is .F.   **e** Although I have some sympathy for this view …
6 Although there is some truth to these ideas A.   **f** A typical assertion is (that) …

12 Rewrite the sentences underlined in 9 using two of the phrases in 11.

13 Write paragraphs for ideas two and three in the plan in 8.
Use different phrases to introduce the benefits.

> **Technique**
>
> Don't write out the rubric of the question in the same words. Reword the question as much as possible and remember that if you copy out the rubric, it won't be included in your word count.

Practice Test 3

Task 1

You should spend about 20 minutes on this task.

The flow chart shows 'trampling', the negative effect of tourists walking in the countryside for the environment. Summarize the information by selecting and reporting the main features.

Write at least 150 words.

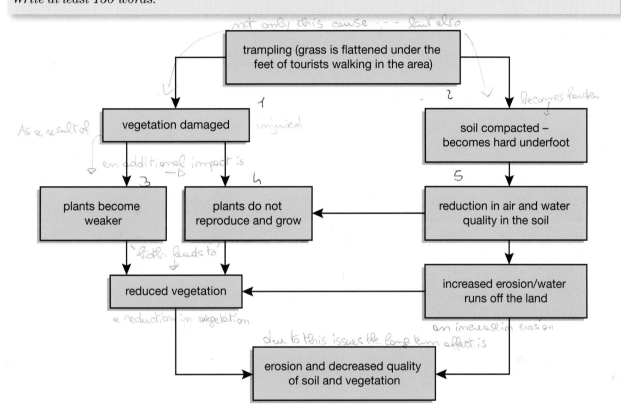

Task 2

You should spend about 40 minutes on this task.

Some young people look forward to a year of travelling, a 'gap year', before they begin work or university and see it as a chance to broaden their horizons. For others this is an expensive waste of time. Discuss both views and give your own opinion.

Write at least 250 words.

Culture

TASK 1	Comparing statistics Using comparatives & superlatives Contrastive linkers & adverbial clauses	**TASK 2**	Vocabulary related to culture Forms for hypothesis and concluding statements Structuring a problem-solving essay

Task 1 Comparing statistics

1 Look at the definitions of high and low culture below. Then name the different cultural activities/places in the pictures. Which would you label 'high culture' and which would you label 'low culture'?

> **High culture** refers to activities, typically arts, considered the highest value by society, especially the elite.
> **Low culture** refers to popular activities, considered less valuable by society.

2 Which of the activities/places in the pictures do you think are the most popular and why? Which do you prefer?

3 How is technology making culture more accessible?

4 You are going to read some sentences about the number of men and women going to different types of musical concert in the USA. Would you prefer to go to an opera, a classical music concert or a pop concert?

5 Look at the tables and read sentences a–f below. Complete 1 and 2.

    1 Label columns A and B *male* or *female* (it is the same for each table).

    2 Match tables 1–3 with the correct title i–iii.

        i) pop **ii)** opera **iii)** classical music

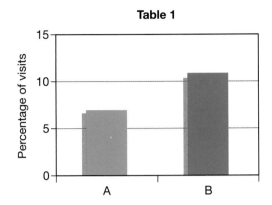

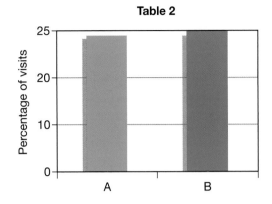

a More females than males went to every event.

b Significantly more women than men went to a classical music event.

c Far fewer people – roughly half the amount – went to see classical music compared to opera.

d Slightly less pop music was listened to by men than women.

e The most popular music event to visit overall was pop.

f Opera concerts were attended by a larger number of people than classical music concerts.

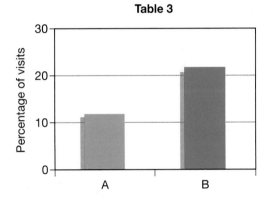

6 Match the sentences a–f from 5 with a sentence below which has the same meaning.

    1 The popularity of pop music was nearly as high with men as with women.

    2 Fewer men than women went to the events shown.

    3 The least popular event was classical music, though opera was also less popular than pop.

    4 Many more people – approximately double – went to see opera compared to classical music.

    5 Far fewer males attended classical music events than females.

    6 A larger majority of people went to opera concerts compared to classical music.

Technique

If there is more than one chart or graph to describe, make sure you check the axes or scales as these could be different for each one. Don't assume they are the same.

---

7 Complete the rules with words from the box.

> adjective (x2) ■ adjectives (x2) ■ considerably ■ countable nouns ■ far
> noun (x2) ■ significantly ■ similarity ■ slightly ■ substantially
> uncountable nouns

1 We can compare _____ using *more/fewer* + _____ + *than*.
2 We can compare _____ using *more/less* + _____ + *than*.
3 We can compare _____ of one syllable using _____ + *-er/-est*.
4 We can compare _____ of two syllables or more using *more/less/the most/*

    the least + _____ .

5 We can show _____ with *as* + adjective + *as*.

6 We can show a small difference by using _____ .

7 We can emphasise a big difference by using _____ , _____ ,

    _____ , _____ and *many/much more*.

8 Find an example for each rule in 7 in the sentences a–f in 5 and sentences 1–6 in 6.

9 The bar chart below shows the percentage of people who use their smartphones to watch television. Write five sentences comparing:
1 age group 18–24 to the other groups.
2 age groups 35–44 and 55–64.
3 age group 65+ to the other groups.
4 age groups 18–24 and 25–34.
5 age groups 55–64 and 25–34.

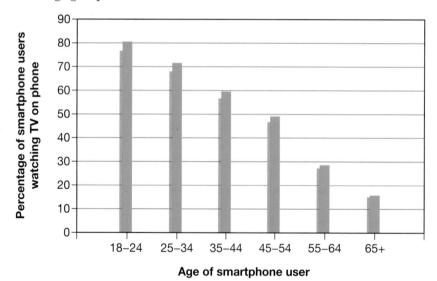

10 Complete the sentences about the chart with the correct age groups.
Of those who watch TV via their phones, …

1 the vast majority are aged _____ to _____ .

2 a small minority are aged _____ .

3 just under 50 per cent are aged _____ to _____.

4 roughly a third are aged _____ to _____ .

5 just over 70 per cent, nearly three-quarters, are aged _____ to _____ .

> **Technique**
> Lists of comparative forms are difficult to read. Vary this with some language using proportions.

11 Read the text below about the chart in 9. Rewrite each underlined phrase 1–7 using a different phrase.

> The bar chart illustrates the number of smartphone users in different age groups who watch television on their phones. The [1] largest number of those who watch television this way, [2] about 80 per cent of the total, come from the 18-to-24 age bracket. In contrast, the group [3] with the minority of users is the 65+ age group. [4] Just under 50 per cent of people aged 45 to 54 used their phones to watch TV, around half of this age group, compared to 60 per cent of those in the age group below. This group is [5] twice the size of the 55-to-64-year-old group, whereas the 25 to 34 year olds were [6] considerably greater in number again, totalling [7] slightly above 70 per cent.

12 Read the text again and find the three words/phrases that compare and contrast information.

  1 i _ c _ _ _ _ _ _ _ _
  2 c _ _ _ _ _ _ _ _ t _
  3 w _ _ _ _ _ _

Technique

Use concession and contrast linkers to make sure sentences flow. As with other linkers, vary the forms and don't overuse them or the good effect will be lost.

13 Match 1–3 in 12 with their synonyms a–c.

  a whilst/while
  b conversely/on the other hand
  c in comparison

14 Add the words from the box to the correct place in the table about adverbial clauses.

although ▪ despite ▪ however ▪ in contrast ▪ in spite of ▪ nevertheless ▪ though whereas ▪ while ▪ whilst

Contrast	Introduces contrasting information	Before contrasting information; followed by subject + verb
		but
		1 _____ **2** _____ **3** _____
		Introduces contrasting information in a new sentence
		4 _____
Concession	Introduces information that seems to oppose what has come before	Before concession; followed by subject + verb
		5 _____ **6** _____
		Before concession; followed by noun or noun phrase
		7 _____ **8** _____
		Before concession to open a new sentence with a subject and verb
		9 _____ **10** _____

15 Look at the pie chart showing why people choose to watch TV on a phone. Complete the sentences using words from exercise 14. More than one answer may be possible.

Reasons for using phones to access television

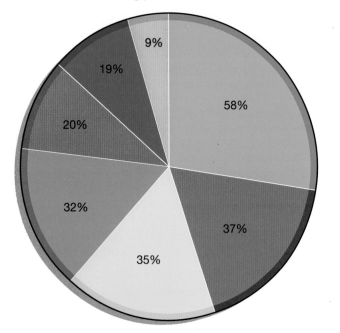

- ☐ Keep busy when ads are on
- ☐ Check if information heard on TV is true
- ☐ Visit a website mentioned on TV
- ☐ Exchange text messages with someone else watching
- ☐ See what others are saying about what you are watching
- ☐ Post comments online about what you are watching
- ☐ Vote for a reality show

Technique

Pie charts are useful tools for comparing proportions. Some pie charts divide an item or activity into completely separate parts which total 100 per cent. Other pie charts show how items or activities overlap – in this case, because some items may appear in two categories, the total can reach more than 100 per cent. In either case the proportions will be easy to compare.

---

1 The largest number of phone users, a total of 58 per cent, use their device to keep busy when there are advertisements _____ the smallest percentage, only 9 per cent, use phones because they want to vote on interactive television programmes.

2 Thirty-five per cent of people watch TV on a phone in order to visit websites that are mentioned on programmes, _____ not for reading reviews of the programme itself: only 20 per cent do this.

3 Almost 40 per cent of people use a phone to stream TV because they want to check that the information is correct. _____ , quite a small number use their phone so they can post comments themselves.

4 _____ the fact that they are watching a programme, 32 per cent use their phone so they can exchange text messages with someone else who is watching.

5 The lowest percentage of people use phones interactively to vote on reality shows. _____ , most other activities depend upon the phone having access to the internet, e.g. to text or visit websites.

Technique

Vary the way you express proportions and remember to include specific numbers for some examples but not every item mentioned, so the writing isn't overwhelmed with detail.

Task 2 Hypothesis and conclusion

1 Add words from the box to the correct category in the table below. Some words fit in more than one category.

> abstract ■ aisle ■ box office ■ curator ■ curtain ■ exhibit ■ film script ■ gig
> microphones ■ painting ■ play (n) ■ portrait ■ projector ■ screen ■ sculpture ■ speakers
> stage ■ support act ■ usher ■ vocalist

art gallery/museum	cinema	music concert	theatre
abstract			

2 Read the statements below. Do you agree or disagree with them? Why?

1 Unless theatre is cheaper, the price of tickets will always be <u>a drawback</u>, preventing it from being as popular as other art forms.
2 Providing that the programmes are of good quality, TV can offer many <u>benefits</u> to children.
3 On condition that they can take entrance fees, museums that charge have <u>an advantage</u> over ones that don't because they have more income to invest.
4 We should censor films and TV to ensure that they have some positive educational <u>uses</u> and do not harm the development of children.
5 Should the general public continue to download films and music illegally, without paying, there will be <u>difficulties</u> in financing future productions.

3 Look at the underlined words in 3. Write a related adjective form for each.

1 a drawback = problematic/disadvantageous

4 Rewrite each sentence in 3 using *if* and the adjectives from 4.

If theatre isn't any cheaper, the price of tickets will always be problematic, preventing it from being as popular as other art forms.

5 The sentences in exercise 3 all use hypothesis.
1 Underline the phrases which replace *if.*
2 Which one creates a negative meaning?

> **Technique**
> Use modal verbs as well as other grammatical structures in order to show hypothesis or lack of certainty.

6 Look at the following Task 1 question. It is a problem-solving essay question. Do you need to suggest solutions or evaluate them?

You should spend about 40 minutes on this task.
How could we encourage people to visit museums more?
Write at least 250 words.

7 Read the model answer then complete the table below.

> Ensuring that visitor numbers to museums are high is an important task at a time when there is a limited amount of money available in the arts. Unless there are sufficient visitors at museums, maintaining them will be problematic and it will be difficult for them to offer interesting exhibitions. In my opinion, this would be a massive drawback in a society that values its cultural heritage. Therefore, it is important to consider how museums might encourage people to visit.
>
> Firstly, it would be useful if museums could provide free entry. Some already do but others charge a fee. Of course, this is a helpful source of income for the museums but if we take the view that culture should be available to everyone, it is logical to suggest that the government should fund each museum. If entry was free, this would immediately encourage more people to go to museums and families would be able to take their children, who may become more enthusiastic about museums in the future, too. Of course, a disadvantage of this is the lost income but if funds could be provided centrally, this wouldn't be a problem.
>
> In addition, provided that it doesn't harm any of the exhibits, more interactive exhibitions would encourage younger people to go to museums. If some interactive activities such as screen-based games were available, it would make the museum accessible to younger visitors. For example, visuals of the exhibits in their original setting or interactive quiz questions could work well. A drawback to this is that it might be expensive to manage but it seems to be worth the investment if it encourages more visitors.
>
> Lastly, unless museums advertise, people won't be aware of what they can offer. For this reason, a good advertising campaign reminding people of how interesting museums are will possibly increase numbers. Although some people feel this might attract people with the wrong attitude or expectations and create noisy crowds within the museum, it is unlikely numbers will grow to the point where they create a hindrance.
>
> In conclusion, museums would benefit from offering up-to-date exhibitions without charging entrance fees and their visitor numbers would increase dramatically.

Suggestion 1 *Museums provide free entry*	Advantage:
	Disadvantage:
Suggestion 2 _____	Advantage:
	Disadvantage:
Suggestion 3 *good advertising*	Advantage: *people will go more*
	Disadvantage: *expectation and wrong kind of people*

Technique

In a problem-solving essay, you will need to brainstorm solutions before writing. Also consider the disadvantages of each solution so that you can mention these, too, giving a more rounded argument.

8 Which word(s) introduce each suggestion?

9 Do the following phrases add information (a) or conclude the ideas (c)? Write (a) or (c).

1 Furthermore
2 To conclude
3 In summary
4 Moreover
5 As well as this/that

Technique

Note down a list of the linkers that you could use in your writing. When you edit, check that you have included a variety of these.

10 Underline the sentences that hypothesize. How many different patterns are there?

11 Look at the following examples from the text in 8 and underline the modal verbs. How would the meaning change if the verbs were changed to *will* or *could?*

In my opinion this would be a massive drawback.

Therefore it is important to consider how museums might encourage people to visit.

Practice Test 4

Task 1

You should spend about 20 minutes on this task.

The graph shows the number of visitors to a variety of art galleries in 2011. Summarize the information by selecting and reporting the main features, and make comparisons where relevant.

Write at least 150 words.

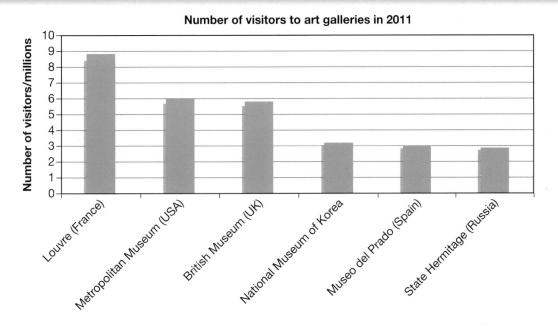

Task 2

You should spend about 40 minutes on this task.

How should we ensure that television is a positive influence in the life of children?

Write at least 250 words.

People
and the environment

TASK 1 Environmental vocabulary
Describing a trend over time
Time expressions

TASK 2 Vocabulary related to buildings
Stating opinions
Giving examples

Task 1 Describing a trend

1 Look at the pictures. Where would you prefer to live? Why?

2 What are the advantages and disadvantages of living in both places?

3 Match 1–5 with a–e to make collocations.

1	over	**a**	generation
2	urban	**b**	areas
3	conservation	**c**	of houses
4	elderly	**d**	population
5	construction	**e**	growth

[handwritten answers:] over population / urban areas/population/growth / conservation of houses/areas / elderly generation/population / construction growth/areas/of houses

4 Complete the sentences with the collocations in 3.

1 In order to meet the demands of a growing population we need to increase the *construction areas* so that people have homes.

2 Higher population numbers in the *elderly generation*, achieved through healthier living and better healthcare, have added to a general increase in population, putting further pressure on housing.

3 If we develop more housing in cities, this could contribute to *urban growth* .

4 However, this is preferable to building in *conservation areas*, which has a negative effect on the environment.

5 If the number of people continues to grow too fast, we will have a situation of *over population*.

5 Do you agree with the sentences in 4? Why/why not?

> **Technique**
>
> Record groups of vocabulary in topics when you note down new words. Add a note of any collocations and related prepositions. You should also record different forms of words (noun/adjective/ verb forms, for example) at the same time as recording the 'key' word.

6 Look at the chart below, which shows changes in rural and urban populations in the world.

1 Draw a line to divide the diagram into three parts: the past, around the current period, the future.

2 What tenses do you need to use to describe each section?

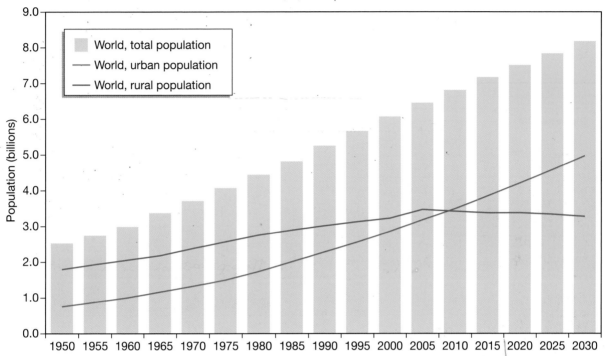

The urban and rural population of the world, 1950–2030

7 Read the paragraph below and answer the questions.

1 What tense is used in the first sentence and why?

2 Underline the section that refers to the past and find the three verbs in the past simple tense.

3 Underline the section that refers to the current period. Which two tenses are used here? Why?

4 Underline the section which talks about the future. Which tenses are used here and why?

> *present perfect*
>
> According to the chart, the urban population of the world has risen steadily since 1950. At that time it was at a level of just under 1 billion people and rose gradually until the year 2000 when the number of people living in cities was roughly double its previous level. It is still increasing now and has been growing more *present continuous* *pres. perfect continuous* rapidly since 2005 when it overtook rural population levels. The numbers of city dwellers are predicted to rise further and it is projected that they will reach just under 5 billion by 2030.

ABITANTI

8 Complete the table below with examples from the paragraph in 7 which relate to the times given.

Time expression	Tense	Example
since 1950	present perfect *Happen in the past effects still effective now*	The urban population of the world has risen steadily
at that time	past simple	it was
the year 2000	pas simple	was
now	present continuous	still increasing
since 2005	present perfect continuous	The pop. has grown since 2005 (P.Perf) the pop. has been growing since 2005 (P.P. cont)
by 2030	future	they will reach

9 Read the final sentence about the urban population again. Rewrite the sentence twice, replacing both underlined verb forms with the alternatives a and b. Use the passive when possible.

The numbers of city dwellers are predicted to rise further and it is projected that they will reach just under 5 billion by 2030.

a likely to/expect

b set/forecast

10 Look at the information about the rural population in the chart in 6. Complete the text below with the correct form of the verbs in brackets.

The rural population of the world [1] has followed (follow) a very slight upward trend overall since 1950. It [2] began (begin) at a level slightly below 2 billion and then [3] increased (increase) marginally until it [4] reached (reach) a peak in 2005. This [5] was maintained (maintain) until 2010. Since then the number of people living in rural communities [6] has fallen (fall) very slightly. It [7] is predicted (predict) to fall slightly further and it [8] is projected (project) that the rural population [9] will drop (drop) further to a level of roughly 3 billion.

11 Match each time expression 1–12 with the tense(s) a–d often used with it.

1 since 1950   B
2 during that period   c
3 in the current period   A
4 … in 2005   c
5 from 1950 to 1970   c
6 from now until 2030   D
7 currently   A
8 in 5 years' time   D
9 by 2050   D
10 between now and 2045   D
11 at the moment   A
12 for the last month   B

a present simple/present continuous
b present perfect
c past simple/past continuous
d future forms

> **Technique**
>
> If the line graph covers a period of time, use your pencil to mark the change from one period to another and divide it into three sections (e.g. past years, the current year and future years). This will remind you to check that your use of tenses is appropriate and accurate.

12 Look at the graph, which shows the population in China, India, Europe and the USA. Write sentences describing 1–7.

1 the trend for all four countries between 1950 and 1960
2 the change for India and China up to 2010
3 the trend for the USA up to 2010
4 the trend for Europe up to 2010
5 the trend for the USA and Europe compared to China and India around the current time
6 the projected trend for China and India by 2050
7 the projected trend for Europe and the USA by 2050

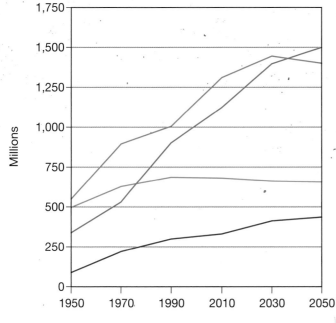

Population growth and projections

— China
— India
— Europe
— USA

Millions

1950 1970 1990 2010 2030 2050

Overall india shows a constent increase in the past from 1950 to 2010 and as predicted by the graph population's rate will continue to grow

Overall the growth of population in india is rising more rapidly now then in the past. Moreover, as is predicted it will continue to rise until 2050 but at a more gradual pace

Task 2 Stating opinions

1 Look at the pictures. Match the buildings a–d with the features 1–5. There may be more than one answer.

   1 pillars or columns
   2 beams
   3 glass windows
   4 a geometric design
   5 many storeys

2 Do you like contemporary or traditional architecture? Why?

3 Look at the Task 2 question below. What type of essay is it?

> *You should spend about 40 minutes on this task.*
>
> **It is more important to use the space in cities well than make them look beautiful. To what extent do you agree?**
>
> *Write at least 250 words.*

4 Look at the plan opposite. The key points 1–11 are listed but one supporting detail for each point is missing. Complete the plan with the correct details a–e.

   a e.g. younger people tend to want to live in city – work opportunities. But housing very expensive – not enough of it.
   b e.g. some companies spend money creating beautiful surroundings – improves productivity; many famous buildings used on tourist websites to attract interest.
   c e.g. megacities – Tokyo, Mexico City, Mumbai – huge. High population and larger areas covered.
   d e.g. roof-top gardens
   e e.g. in Dubai tallest building created

Introduction

1 Cities: have high density of buildings. c

2 *megacities -Tokyo Mexico city, Mumbai - huge. High population end larger areas covered.*

3 I partly agree that space needs to be used well. *end larger areas covered.*

Reason 1 – agree because

4 Important to use space effectively – population of world increasing/more people need to live in cities A

5 *Younger people tend to want to live in city - work opportunities. But housing very expensive - not enough of it*

Reason 2 – agree because

6 Design of high-rise architecture suitable for buildings in city – buildings in cities generally contemporary and high rise – economic use of space e

7 *In Dubai talles building created*

Reason 1 – disagree because B

8 Attractive surroundings improve quality of life/attract tourists and income

9 *Some companies spend money creating beautiful surroundings - improves productivity; many famous buildings used on tourist websites to attract interest.*

Reason 2 – disagree because

10 Nowadays good design includes green space but still economic – also better for environment

11 *Roof-top gardens*

Conclusion

Agree space is important but not the only factor to consider.

Technique

Decide on your viewpoint before you begin. This helps you present the information consistently throughout the essay. Remember your adverbs, introductory phrases and general language should indicate your attitude, not just the introduction and conclusion of your essay.

5 It is important to distinguish between opinions you hold and those that are more general. Look at each statement in the plan in 4 and decide if it is a generally accepted opinion (g) or an opinion held by the writer specifically (w). Write (g) or (w).

6 Read the introduction and first paragraph of a model answer below. Underline the phrases that introduce opinions.

It is generally accepted that contemporary cities are growing in size and population. Various recent reports have indicated growth in megacities such as Mumbai, Tokyo and Mexico City, which cover huge areas and are still developing. Along with the increase in population globally, it is therefore commonly acknowledged that there is pressure on available space and housing. I would therefore maintain that space is an important factor in city planning and must be taken into account in any kind of planning activity. However, although space is key to good city design, it is not the only thing that should be considered and this essay will go on to discuss other factors, too.

To begin with, a primary factor for consideration is population. Experts claim that the population of the world is increasing quickly and it is true that urban societies are growing very rapidly. More young people, for instance, are moving to cities for work opportunities as well as all the facilities and opportunities they can find there. For this reason, I believe we need to find more economic ways to live. Good design, with high-rise living space, can help. It seems to me that the cost of accommodation in many cities is prohibitive, which restricts opportunities and could be solved by better town planning.

Technique

When writing an opinion essay you need to present different viewpoints. These can be varied to appear personal or impersonal. Both are possible approaches.

7 Add the underlined phrases from 6 to the correct place in the table below.

Personal opinion	Impersonal idea
I think I'm my opinion to my mind As far as I'm concerned Personally, I'm certain I feel (that)	It should be noted that It's claimed that Many might claim Reports/show/state/demonstrate/reveal that A general assertion is / Prediction suggest that

8 Add the phrases 1–12 to the correct place in the table in 7.

1 I think
2 In my opinion
3 It should be noted that
4 It is claimed that
5 To my mind
6 Many might claim
7 As far as I'm concerned
8 Reports show/state/demonstrate/reveal that
9 Personally, I am certain
10 A general assertion is
11 Predictions suggest that
12 I feel (that)

PERSONAL OPINION
IMPERSONAL IDEA

9 Match 1–6 with a–f to make sentences.

1 Personally, I feel that green spaces in the city C
2 It is commonly accepted that more A
3 Many might claim that they D
4 It seems to me E
5 In my opinion B
6 It should be noted that some cities F

> **Technique**
>
> Giving supporting details or examples is key to strengthening your argument. But use a variety of methods to introduce the evidence or examples.

a housing would make homes more affordable for people such as key workers.
b major cities, Istanbul or Shanghai for instance, are relatively expensive places to live.
c make them nicer places. In other words they make cities healthier and more beautiful.
d enjoy the benefits of the countryside, for example the fresh air, but others would say it is too boring.
e that work opportunities are better in cities. That is to say you have more chance of finding a job.
f are known as megacities due to their size. A case in point is Tokyo.

10 Do you agree or disagree with the sentences in 9?

11 In each sentence in 9 there is an example. The phrases a–f below introduce examples. Answer the questions 1–4.

Which …

1 two phrases are used to repeat and clarify the information?
2 phrase gives a single, exact example?
3 phrase precedes a noun?
4 two phrases are general and can be followed by subject or a verb?

a for example
b for instance
c such as
d in other words
e That is to say
f a case in point is

12 Choose the correct phrase from a–f in 11 to complete the sentences.

1 I love flowers _____ roses.

2 Flowers are beautiful. _____ the rose, which is often used for weddings.

3 We should have more greenery in towns and cities. _____ city planners should try to include gardens in their designs.

4 If old buildings, _____ abandoned houses or shops, are empty, they should be used for homeless people.

5 I love old buildings, _____ medieval houses and bridges. I find it interesting to consider their history.

Practice Test 5

Task 1

You should spend about 20 minutes on this task.

average length of life

The graph shows the life expectancy of people living in Asian regions from 1950 and predicts life expectancy until 2300. Summarize the information by selecting and reporting the main features, and make comparisons where relevant.

Write at least 150 words.

Life expectancy at birth, Asian regions: 1950–2300

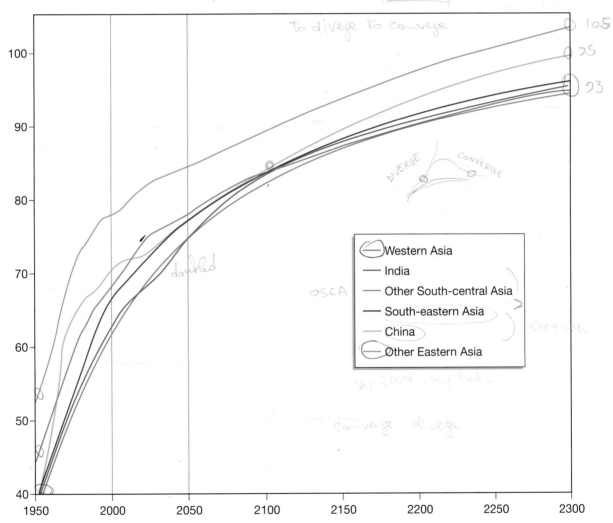

Task 2

You should spend about 40 minutes on this task.

Traffic congestion is becoming increasingly problematic in major cities. What solutions can you suggest to help solve the problem?

Write at least 250 words.

6

Food
and the environment

UNIT AIMS

TASK 1 Food and nutrition vocabulary
Expressing purpose
Structure of a flow
chart essay

TASK 2 Giving reasons
Ordering an 'evaluating solutions'
essay
Referencing to avoid repetition

Task 1 Expressing purpose

1 What is your favourite type of food? What food do you dislike?

2 List two or three dishes that are traditional in your country and two or three that have been 'imported' from other places. Answer the questions.

- Are they similar or different?
- How healthy are they?
- How popular are they?
- How much do they cost?

3 Do you think the types of food people eat will change in the future? Why/why not?

4 Complete the diagram with words and phrases from the box. You can use two items twice.

> balanced ■ comfort ■ confectionery ■ convenience ■ crash ■ delicious
> factory farming ■ fast/junk food ■ free-range ■ intensive farming ■ obesity
> organic farming ■ macrobiotic ■ pesticides ■ savoury ■ sensible
> sustainable agriculture ■ starvation ■ (un)healthy

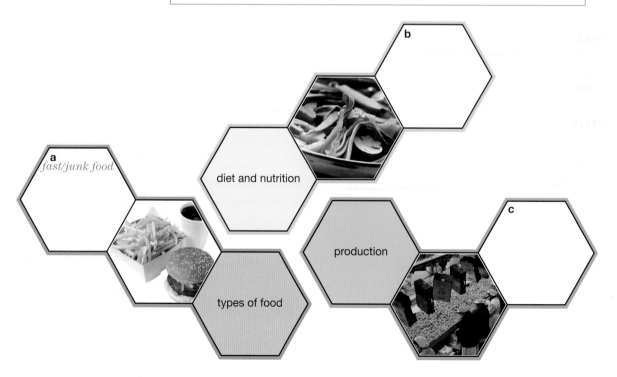

a fast/junk food

b

diet and nutrition

c

production

types of food

5 Read the description and look at the pictures, which show how vegetables are prepared and packaged before they are sold. Number the pictures in the correct order to create a flow chart.

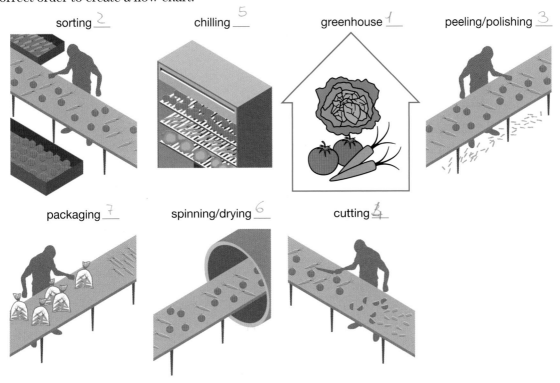

sorting _2_   chilling _5_   greenhouse _1_   peeling/polishing _3_

packaging _7_   spinning/drying _6_   cutting _4_

The flow chart identifies how vegetables and fruit are cleaned and prepared for sale.

There are a number of different stages undertaken in order to ensure that the vegetables are in the correct condition for the shops. These include cleaning, cutting and packaging.

The first stage of the process begins when the vegetables and fruit are picked and taken out of the greenhouse. Having been collected, they are subsequently sorted by hand so as to remove any that are below standard. Those that are good enough are then polished or peeled depending on the type of vegetable or fruit they are. Similarly, some are also pre-cut for market. Next all the vegetables and fruit are put through a process of chilling to keep them fresh. After this initial chilling, the produce is put through a spinning machine so that it is dry. Finally the end product is packaged in order that it meets the standards required for selling.

In summary, the process of preparation ensures that vegetables and fruit are all cleaned, cut as necessary and packaged so that they are in good condition and can be sold in shops and supermarkets.

6 Answer the questions below.

1 Match the sections a–d with the content i–iv.

IV **a** introduction   **i** clarifies the parts of the process more specifically

I   **b** first paragraph   **ii** gives detailed information about each part of the process

II **c** second paragraph   **iii** general overall statement made about the complete process

III **d** conclusion   **iv** identifies the type of information shown in the flow chart overall

2 Find an example of a participle clause in the text in 5.

3 Find some examples of 'signposting' language in the text in 5.

> **Technique**
>
> If the question in Part 1 is about a process, you still need to make a plan for this. Does the process have different stages or phases? How many? You should include an overview of this.

7 Complete the sentences using words and phrases from the text in 5.

1 There are a number of different stages undertaken _____ ensure the vegetables are in the correct condition.

2 They are sorted by hand _____ remove any that are below standard.

3 Some are pre-cut _____ market.

4 They are put through a process of chilling _____ keep them fresh.

5 The produce is put through a spinning machine _____ it is dry.

6 The product is packaged _____ it meets the standards required for selling.

8 Look at the words and phrases in the gaps in 7. Which function do they have?

9 Complete the table using words and phrases from 7.

Expressing purpose	Structure
1 _____	+ infinitive verb
2 _____	
3 _____	
4 _____	+ noun/gerund
5 _____	+ subject and verb (clause)
6 _____	

10 Match 1–5 with a–e to make sentences about farmers' markets, where farmers sell their produce directly to people.

1 Originally, people farmed land

2 Eventually farmers' markets evolved

3 Often the farmers would go to a central

4 Farmers' markets declined when

5 Recent interest in organic food has led to

a larger numbers of farmers' markets again, opened so that people can get fresh or organic produce.

b so as to feed themselves and their families.

c to sell the produce to others as well.

d square in order to sell their products.

e people chose supermarkets for their shopping.

11 Look at the flow chart, which shows the first industrial process for making dough. Then answer the questions.

Technique

When you look at a process or flow chart, at the planning stage think about the tools, equipment or ingredients involved, how many parts of the process there are and the cause and effect relationship of each part.

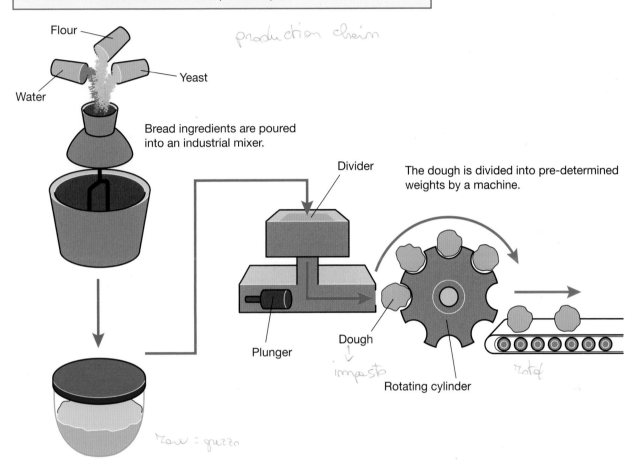

Flour

Yeast

Water

production chain

Bread ingredients are poured into an industrial mixer.

Divider

The dough is divided into pre-determined weights by a machine.

Plunger

Dough
Impasto

Rotating cylinder

Rotd

Raw = grezzo

The dough is fermented naturally or by adding additives.

1 Write a sentence to describe what the flow chart shows.
2 Write two sentences describing a) the ingredients and b) the main parts of the process.
3 Write a sentence describing:
   a why the ingredients are put into an industrial mixer.
   b why additives are added.
   c why the dough is put into a divider.
4 Write a summary of the whole process.

Technique

The ideas you present must be relevant and clear and cover each element of the process. Tick each part of the flow chart once you have included it to check this happens. You won't have time to put in a lot of detail but if you miss a step of the process, the description won't be logical.

Task 2 Giving reasons

1 Look at the pictures of farming methods. What similarities and differences can you identify?

2 How do the words in each set 1–4 connect to each other?

  1 deforestation → soil erosion → less food production

  2 global warming → unreliable rainfall → poor crops

  3 war → farming prevented → imports and exports prevented

  4 rising prices → less available food → starvation

3 Read the sentences and check you understand the meaning of the words in *italics*.

  1 Eating *wholefoods* and natural produce is important for me. They are healthier than other foods.

  2 Intensive farming increases the use of pesticides and *chemical fertilizers*. I prefer to shop at a farmers' market where the food is usually locally produced and organic.

  3 *Genetically modified* crops are crucial I think. They help to prevent starvation, producing much greater quantities of crops.

  4 *Overgrazing* and *deforestation* mean there is less land for food production. Farmers and landowners should be banned from allowing this.

  5 Developed countries should focus on solutions for *climate change*. This issue has a great impact on food production in developing countries.

4 Change each sentence in 3, if necessary, so that it is true for you. Think about why the sentences are/are not true for you.

5 Read the following sentences and underline the conjunction in each.

  a As wholefoods are healthier than other foods, eating natural produce is important for me.

  b Eating natural produce is important for me because wholefoods are healthier than others.

  c Since wholefoods and natural produce are healthier than other types, eating them is important for me.

6 Rewrite sentences 2–5 in 3. In each case use a different conjunction.

> ### Technique
> When you need to give reasons, you can show this by extending the structure of your sentence using linkers.

7 Look at the Task 1 question below. Is it asking you to find solutions or evaluate a solution?

> *You should spend about 40 minutes on this task.*
> **Some people believe that famine is caused by climate change and preventing this will stop famine. What is your view of this?**
> *Write at least 250 words.*

8 Look at the introduction and conclusion of the essay. Put the sentences in the correct order.

Introduction

a Some people believe this is the result of climate change and the impact it has on farming and the ability of less-developed countries to produce sufficient food.

b Famine is a terrible problem which astonishingly still exists in the 21st century.

c Indeed, millions of people still die from starvation every year.

d However, I will argue that, whilst this is one factor which contributes to the problem of famine, there are other causes which have as much impact and must also be considered.

Conclusion

a In summary, what is needed is for a range of causes to be tackled, and global warming is only one of them.

b Politics, economics and technology also have a part to play.

c Whilst global warming is a significant contributor to the problem, and addressing it would also help prevent famine, this alone would not end famine.

d There are clearly many factors involved in the causes of famine.

9 An essay which evaluates solutions often describes the proposed solution and looks at the disadvantages and the advantages. Read paragraph 1 of the essay below. What order do these three elements appear in?

> Of course the impact of climate change can't be underestimated in relation to famine. Climate change is, in itself, caused by many different factors including deforestation and polluted air. The ¹*deforestation problem* leads to soil erosion. The ²*polluted air problem* increases temperatures. ³*Deforestation and polluted air* contribute to unpredictable rainfall patterns which damage crops and the quality of vegetation that grows, preventing steady food production in developing countries. Farmers in ⁴*developing countries* usually don't have enough money for measures which will help counteract the effects, e.g. anti-flooding or irrigation methods. Consequently, preventing climate change would decrease ⁵*climate change's* unpredictable effects and therefore reduce famine. Agricultural planning would be easier as farmers would know what the likely seasonal changes would be. However, climate change is a vast problem and not ⁶*a problem* easily solved. ⁷*The problem* requires a global effort and huge investment, which is difficult to achieve quickly in the short term.

10 What problem can you see in the writing?

11 Replace the words in *italics* 1–7 in the text in 9 with the words below. Read the paragraph again. What is the effect?

   a It   **b** former   **c** such places   **d** the   **e** latter   **f** one   **g** Both of these

12 Match the reference words a–f with the definitions 1–7. You can use some words more than once.

1 replaces a singular noun at the end of the previous sentence

2 replaces a plural noun at the end of a previous sentence

3 replaces a process or situation

4 replaces the first noun in the preceding sentence when there are two

5 replaces the last noun in the preceding sentence when there are two

6 combines with 'as this/as these' or similar to replace a repeated noun

7 replaces the article before a preceding noun

a they/these

b one

c the latter

d it/this

e such

f the former

13 Read paragraph 2 of the essay. Does it evaluate the same solution as paragraph 1 or offer and evaluate an alternative solution?

> Alongside climate change, politics is an important issue to consider when looking at famine. The decisions of political parties and the impact of wars heavily affects the likelihood of famine. In some parts of India, for example, it was a consistent problem until independence was declared. After this it halted. War means that scarce resources are spent on weapons or armies and not invested in farming. Such approaches prevent farmers from long-term planning and managing their land in a normal way. Consequently, preventing war would also prevent famine. In other words, having control over unstable political systems and influence over the processes of war would allow governments to formulate more stable agricultural policies. However, managing these types of changes is demanding and it is unrealistic to suggest that this is achievable, at least for now.

14 Look at the underlined words in paragraph 2 and draw a line to show which noun each one refers to.

15 Complete the next part of the essay with suitable reference words, to avoid repetition.

> Finally, the use of technology could have an influence on when and how often famine happens. [1] _This_ is an important factor because [2] _it_ can help to improve the situation long-term by offering some control to the people of the countries affected. For example, if [3] _this/those_ people were able to access water pumps to irrigate [4] _their_ farms, they may be able to avoid losing crops. Also, food technology and improved food distribution could allow people to manage long-term planning better. [5] _This_ approach takes [6] _the_ issue out of the hands of politicians and does not depend upon climate change being solved.

16 Read the notes for the final part of the essay. Write them out using reference words, to avoid repetition.

> Technology – difficult, requires economic investment. Some money for water pumps, etc. raised through charity but often limited. However, of all solutions this one viable immediately.

In conclusion, the use of technology could help to solve problems of famine but it is difficult to put in place because of the high economic investment required such as the money needed for buying water pumps and so on. However this could be raised through charity but often collections with this way is limited. Despite the difficulties this potential solution seems to be the most viable and immediate solution.

the money available to / raised by charities

Technique

Leave time at the end of your essay to check it through and think about repetition. You will be graded on the range of language you use. Constant repetition suggests that your range is limited, so try to avoid it. Using reference words shows good control of language.

Practice Test 6

Task 1

You should spend about 20 minutes on this task.

where the fish is caught

The diagram shows the process for labelling shellfish for the international market. Summarize the information by selecting and reporting the main features.

Write at least 150 words.

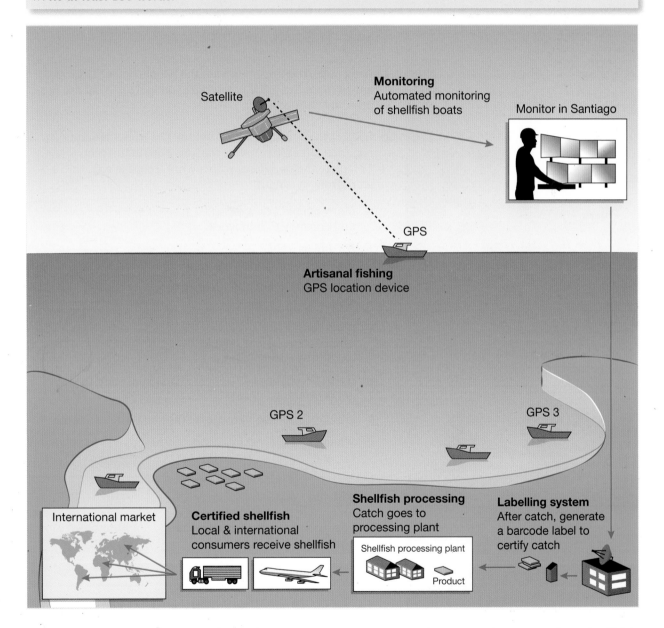

Task 2

You should spend about 40 minutes on this task.

Poor nutrition and obesity is a problem in many developed countries and some people believe that a tax on fast food would reduce the problem. Do you agree?

Write at least 250 words.

The working world

TASK 1 Work collocations	**TASK 2** Fronting sentences
Participle phrases	Opinion phrases
Identifying exceptions	Commonly used language

UNIT AIMS

Task 1 Participle phrases

1 Look at the pictures. What are the people doing? Do you do any of these things? If not, would you like to? What are the pros and cons of each?

2 Look at the collocation grid below. The words around the edge can fit before or after the key word in the centre. Complete the sentences with a word from the edge and a word from the centre.

a Many people are *workshy* and don't try to find work.

b Having friendly _____ is important for job satisfaction.

c A _____ in the Middle East is Sunday to Thursday.

d Nursing requires people to do _____ as nurses have to be on duty at nights sometimes.

e If you have a heavy _____ , it is important to be organized to deal with it.

f If a _____ is comfortable, the staff will be happier.

g When children reach _____ , they should learn about tax and pension systems.

h _____ is not always rewarded with high wages.

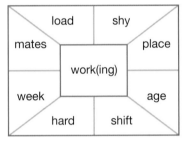

load	shy
mates	place
week	age
hard	shift

work(ing)

3 Do you agree with the sentences in 2? Why/why not?

4 Create two more collocation grids in your notebook. Write the key words *job* and *salary* in the centre of the grids. Add correct words from the box below around the edge of each grid. One word fits both grids.

> ### Technique
> You should try to include collocations in your writing to show that you understand natural phrasing in English.

> annual ■ apply for ■ competitive ■ full ■ final ■ high
> high-powered ■ hold down ■ increase ■ manual ■ permanent
> safeguard ■ satisfaction ■ skilled ■ starting

5 Choose three collocations from each grid. Write a sentence with each which is true for you.

6 Complete the sentences using the correct form of collocations from 4.

1 Not having income from a/an _____ , many older people have to rely on a pension to live.

2 Arriving at the office, she noticed another candidate who had _____ the job already sitting outside the interview room.

3 The company closed down its factory, leaving many of those doing _____ without employment.

4 Given enough time, she will get promoted into a _____ and no doubt will be a huge success.

5 The teacher, enjoying the _____ gained from doing something she loves, is new to the area.

6 Before getting a more _____ , he had to achieve an excellent report.

7 Look at the sentences in 6 again and underline the participle clauses.

8 Look at the six types of participle clause below and the examples. Match sentences 1–6 in 6 with a type a–f.

Type	Full clause	Participle clause
a to give a reason	She couldn't apply for the job as she wasn't qualified.	Not being qualified, she couldn't apply for the job.
b to show a condition	If the pay is sufficiently competitive, the job will attract good applicants.	Given sufficiently competitive pay, the job will attract good applicants.
c to give a result	The value of the company rose with the result that the owners made a considerable profit.	The value of the company rose, making the owners a considerable profit.
d to show a time	While the manager made his speech, he showed a set of PowerPoint slides.	Making his speech, the manager showed a set of PowerPoint slides.
e to replace a relative clause	The accountant, who was doing extra hours, managed to complete all the accounts in time.	The accountant, having done extra hours, managed to complete all the accounts in time.
f after a preposition	After he had reached the age of 75, the chairman retired.	After reaching the age of 75, the chairman retired.

9 Read the pairs of sentences and answer the questions.

1 a Doing such a bad interview, I don't think I will get the job.
  b Doing such a bad interview, I didn't think I would get the job.
  Which sentence is in the past? Does the participle clause tell us this or the main verb?

2 a Organized properly for the meeting, the office looked much better.
  b Having been organized properly for the meeting, the office looked much better.
  Which sentence emphasises the order of the actions?

3 a They advertised their business, founded the previous month, on the internet.
  b Advertising the product on the internet worked well.
  Which sentence has an active meaning and which has a passive meaning?

10 Rewrite the sentences a–e using participle clauses.

    a Because she got such excellent qualifications, she didn't have problems getting her first job.

    _____

    b After he had graduated, he spent some time on a gap year.

    _____

    c My manager, who has just given in his notice, wants me to leave too and work with him.

    _____

    d Provided that the job is completed step by step, it won't be difficult.

    _____

    e While the teacher had offered a lot of help, she still encouraged her student to work autonomously.

    _____

11 Look at the Task 1 question below and pick out three key trends from the line graph.

> _You should spend about 20 minutes on this task._
>
> **The line graph shows the number of people in work per retired pensioner in the UK.**
>
> **Summarize the information by selecting and reporting the main features, and make comparisons where necessary.**
>
> _Write at least 150 words._

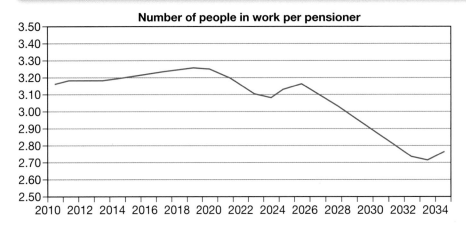

Number of people in work per pensioner

12 Read the model answer below. Does the model answer contain the key trends you picked out in 11?

> The line graph identifies the number of people in work in relation to those who have retired, [1]_and makes_ a projection about the situation up to 2034. The overall trend is likely to be downward bar some short periods where the numbers may rise again. Certainly, by the end of the period the ratio is predicted to be significantly lower than the start, [2]_and it will hit_ its lowest level of just above 2.70 in 2033.
>
> The ratio of working people to pensioners began approximately 0.5 higher than this low point, with 3.18 workers per pensioner in 2010. There was an immediate though minor increase in the next four years, [3]_when it rose_ to just over 3.20.
>
> [4]_After it has reached_ a high of 3.25 by 2020, it is predicted that the ratio will then rapidly decrease with the exception of two years between 2024 and 2026, when it will shoot up again.

13 Replace each underlined phrase 1–4 in the model answer in 12 with a participle phrase.

> **Technique**
> When writing about data, you should show that you understand what the axes or pie chart figures represent. If you don't identify what the numbers refer to (e.g. it rose from 2 to 20; it rose from 2 per cent to 20 per cent), your answer will be unclear or incomplete.

14 Look at the first paragraph of the model answer in 12 again and complete the sentence below.

The overall trend is likely to be downward _____ some short periods where the numbers may rise again.

15 Which of the following words/phrases cannot replace the word in the gap in 14?

> except for ▪ other than ▪ unless ▪ with the exception of ▪ without

16 Look at the sets of information 1–4 and complete the sentences.

   1 **a** a half   **b** a third   **c** three-quarters
      d 30 per cent

      All the quantities are fractions <u>except for</u> d which _____ .

   2 **a** 0.5   **b** 1.4   **c** 4   **d** 54.5

      None of the examples are whole numbers <u>other than</u> _____ .

   3 **a** nearly 20   **b** significantly less than 20   **c** far less than 20
      d noticeably lower than 20

      The quantities are all much lower than 20 <u>with the exception of</u> _____ .

   4 **a** 50 per cent   **b** half   **c** part   **d** 0.5

      The quantities are all related in amount <u>bar</u> _____ .

17 Using one of the underlined phrases from 16, complete the sentences. Use your own ideas.

   1 Commuters often travel …
   2 Work is …
   3 Dangerous jobs are …

> **Technique**
> However good the language in your answer, you must also interpret the data correctly and ensure that you give accurate information.

Task 2 Fronting sentences

1 What do you know about child labour?

2 Read the paragraph about child labourers and answer the questions below.

   a Do we know for sure the exact numbers of children working in slave-like conditions?

   b What are the conditions for children like generally?

   c Which fact is particularly worrying?

   d Why is it possible for this to happen?

A number of well-known charities claim that millions of people in the world work in slave-like conditions, including children. One such charity, Compassion, suggests that one in six children between age 5 and 14 in developing countries is involved in work of some kind. This rises to 30 per cent in the least developed countries. Whilst statistics are not exact and can be refuted, there seems to be convincing evidence that slavery amongst children is a significant problem. Working children often labour in hazardous conditions and suffer cruelty and beatings. More disturbing still are the 22 000 children each year who die in work-related accidents. Most children work in the informal sector, e.g. in homes or on the streets where they have no legal protection. Also unprotected are the 49 million children, the highest proportion globally, who work in sub-Saharan Africa, often in terrible conditions.

3 What are the possible causes for child labour? Think about the ideas below.

   a poverty

   b tradition

   c culture

   d social support

   e orphans

4 In the paragraph in 2, underline the sentence about the children who work in sub-Saharan Africa. Do you notice anything about the structure of the sentence and the position of the subject?

5 The sentences 1–4 contain examples of 'fronting'. Match each sentence with a pattern a–d.

   1 Much more shocking is the fact that 73 million working children are younger than 10 years old.

   2 So shocking are these figures that charities across the world are attempting to find solutions to the problem.

   3 Standing behind the problem, however, are world governments who need to listen to concerned charities.

   4 Outraged the charities may be, but without the action of governments change will be hard.

   a object/complement of sentence or clause in subject position

   b superlative/comparative + *be* + subject

   c adverbial phrase of position/movement + *be* + subject

   d *such/so/also* + adjective + *be* + subject

Technique

Formal writing often uses less typical sentence structure to add emphasis. If you can use these forms accurately, it will make your writing more sophisticated.

6 Make the following sentences emphatic by 'fronting' them using the patterns a–d in 5.

   1 The amount of time spent at work is so high that people often suffer from stress-related illnesses.

   2 The manager, who was standing at the front of the meeting, announced some redundancies.

   3 Employees are so satisfied with the opportunities to progress in the business that they don't leave the company.

   4 Social work was much more exciting than his previous role in banking.

   5 The job might be badly paid but it provides a high level of job satisfaction.

Useful typical language

7 Look at some sentences from the paragraph in 2 and underline the words or phrases which express an attitude or opinion rather than fact.

   a Charities claim that millions of people in the world work in slave-like conditions.

   b Compassion suggests that one in six children between age 5 and 14 in developing countries is involved in work.

   c Statistics are not exact and can be refuted.

   d … there seems to be convincing evidence that slavery amongst children is a significant problem.

8 Look at the words and phrases you underlined in 7 and answer the questions.

   a Which are verbs and which are adjective + noun forms?

   b Which of the verbs are used actively and which is used passively?

9 Put the reporting verbs from 7 (*claim, suggest, refute*) into the correct category in the diagram below.

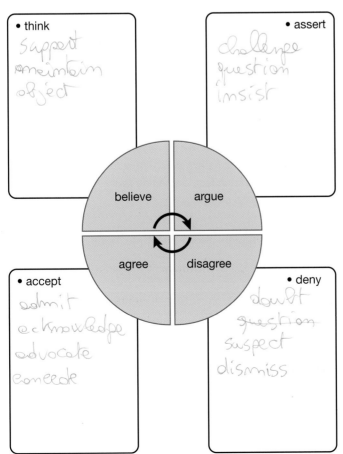

- think
  support
  maintain
  object

- assert
  challenge
  question
  insist

- accept
  admit
  acknowledge
  advocate
  concede

- deny
  doubt
  question
  suspect
  dismiss

believe   argue

agree   disagree

10 Add the verbs from the box to the correct category in the diagram in 9.

> acknowledge ■ admit ■ advocate ■ challenge ■ concede ■ dismiss ■ doubt ■ insist
> maintain ■ object ■ question ■ support ■ suspect

11 Look at some other typical verb, adjective and noun forms used in IELTS essays. Circle the option which is <u>not</u> possible in each case.

a This argument can be *rejected/refuted/denied/conceded* due to the strong opposing evidence.

b Such a viewpoint can be *supported/refused/defended/backed* as there is a convincing argument to support it.

c This idea is simply *conjecture/speculation/proof/theoretical* and not proven.

d The prevailing opinion is *debatable/compelling/almost unanimous/convincing* so most people agree with it.

e This stance is based on *a misconception/a misunderstanding/hearsay/reasoned evidence* and can be easily disproved.

f It is *true/unarguable/unclear/commonly recognized* that this is so.

g This *source/opinion/attitude/viewpoint* is commonly held by many.

h Such a/an *issue/concern/matter/item* is controversial.

i Many people disagree with this *situation/state/ailment/circumstance*.

j A/An *important/crucial/heavy/vital* factor is the following.

12 Look at the Task 2 question and the start of an introduction to the essay below. Underline three reporting verbs in the introduction which express opinion.

> *You should spend about 40 minutes on this task.*
>
> **Many believe that doing a part-time job can be beneficial to children and help them develop into better adults. Why is this? Give reasons for your answers and include any relevant examples from your own knowledge or experience.**
>
> *Write at least 250 words.*

> Children below the age of 16 have often undertaken part-time jobs in many countries, doing a few hours' work each week to earn some pocket money. Some people assert that this is not a key issue because it doesn't have a great impact on children while others object strongly, maintaining that it is, in fact, damaging and takes up time and energy the children could better spend studying.

13 Read the question in 12 again. Think of one or two facts about this topic and make notes.

Children – legally allowed to work in my country at the age of 14. Only for a few hours per week.

14 Think of two or three commonly held ideas or opinions for or against the statement in the question in 12.

Most people think work experience = useful/good for understanding reality of work.

15 Use your notes in 13 and 14 to write 2–3 sentences. Use vocabulary from 10 or 11 in each sentence.

It is unarguable that children can in fact work in my country after the age of 14 although only for very short periods per week.
The idea that children benefit from having experience of the realities of work is compelling.

> **Technique**
>
> You can make notes on your answer sheet including quick lists of different vocabulary to help you vary the range you use. Cross them out cleanly at the end to ensure they are not assessed.

Practice Test 7

Task 1

You should spend about 20 minutes on this task.

The graph shows the number of fatal injuries (resulting in death) of workers in New Zealand between 1992 and 2010.

Summarize the information by selecting and reporting the main features, and make comparisons where relevant.

Write at least 150 words.

Number of fatal work injuries, 1992–2010

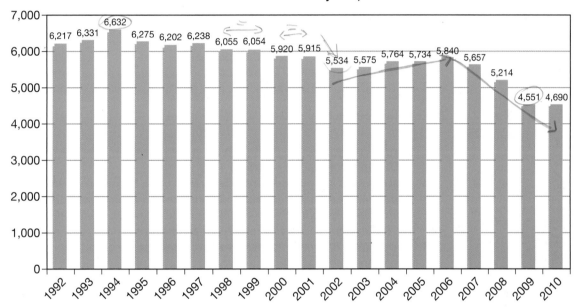

Task 2

You should spend about 40 minutes on this task.

Some people believe that it would be beneficial if employees worked three or four days per week rather than five or six days.

Why is this? Give reasons for your answers and include any relevant examples from your own knowledge or experience.

Write at least 250 words.

8

Sports
and activities

UNIT AIMS

TASK 1   Spelling errors
          Sporting vocabulary
          Finding correlations

TASK 2   Word class
          Relative clauses
          Ordering a conclusion

Task 1 Finding correlations

1 Read the sentences about why sport can be positive and number them in order of importance for you. 1 = most important, 5 = least important. Think about why.

   a Sport helps develop coordination and balance.

   b It is very good for health to do exercise.

   c Sport allows people to learn about competition in a positive way.

   d Children who are less academic may find they can excel in sports.

2 Read the sentences about why sport can be negative. In each sentence there are two spelling errors. Correct each error.

   a Sport may be beneficil for health but it also results in many people suffering from sports injuries.

   b When people are very commited fans, they often become too passionate about their team and this means supportors can clash, especially in football.

   c Competition in sport is very usefull for children who need to learn about life, but if they don't get positive advise it can encourage them to be aggressive.

   d The amount of money earned by sports stars has gradualy increased and is now far too high, meaning that sport is now a business without sufficent focus on the competition itself.

   e Exceling at sports requires a lot of practice; if young people spend too much time on this, they may neglect school work and recieve poor grades.

3 Do you agree with the sentences in 2? Why/why not?

4 Look at the pictures of sports below. Write the name of each sport in the appropriate box.

a	**b**	**c**	**d**

swimming • •	• •	• •	• •

5 Add two words from the box below to each box in 4. One word is for the place where the sport happens and one is for the equipment.

> clubs ■ course ■ court ■ goal ■ goggles ■ pitch ■ pool ■ racquet

6 Look at the information below about heat-related illness in sports activities and answer the questions.

The bar chart shows the number of heat-related illnesses suffered by high school students per 100 000 sports events in central US states. The line graph shows the average temperatures for one year in a central US state.

a Can you see any similarities in pattern?
b What kind of link between the two sets of information does this suggest?
c Are there any areas that do not link in the way you might expect?

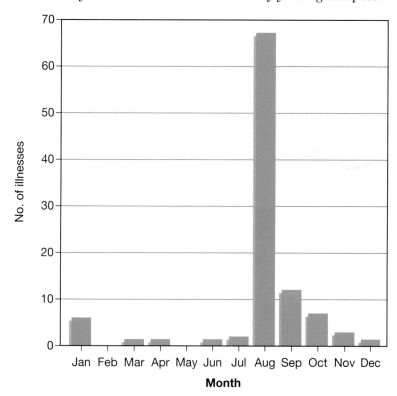

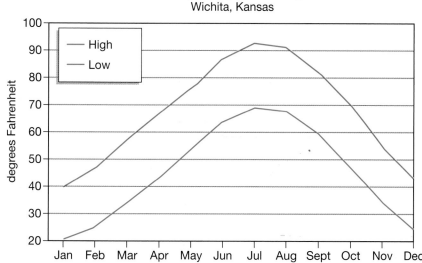

Average temperature range
Wichita, Kansas

7 Read the model answer below. How is the essay structured?

The bar chart shows the number of students from high school who were affected by heat-related illnesses in one year when participating in sports events in central US states. The line graph shows the average temperature in Fahrenheit over a year for one of those states. When considered together, the information suggests that there was a ¹ <u>link</u> between temperature and the number of illnesses suffered by sports participants, but this was not consistent.

The ² <u>vast</u> majority of illnesses occurred in August, reaching a peak at ³ <u>just under</u> 70 incidences per 100 000 sporting events. This number was at a ⁴ <u>much</u> higher level than at any other point in the year, almost seven times that of September, which experienced the next highest occurrence. It also correlates with a similar peak in temperature, which reached ⁵ <u>approximately</u> 92 degrees Fahrenheit in the same month at its highest and 69 degrees Fahrenheit at its lowest.

However, in the winter months, the numbers of heat-related illnesses and the temperatures did not follow similar proportional trends. Temperatures dropped steadily from August to December, dipping to a minimum of 20 degrees Fahrenheit and remaining there for January and February. However, illnesses reached their minimum of zero in February and May when the temperatures were at 25 degrees Fahrenheit and 55 degrees Fahrenheit respectively. There was actually a minor increase in the number of illnesses in January to roughly seven, when temperatures were at their lowest point for the whole year.

Overall the figures suggest a possible association between very high temperatures in the summer and the number of heat-related illnesses, but the correlation is not consistent at other times of the year.

8 Replace the underlined phrases in the model answer in 7 with the expressions a–e.

a far/significantly/substantially
b connection
c roughly/more or less
d overall/overwhelming
e almost/about

9 Which 3 phrases in paragraphs 2–4 (not underlined) in the model answer are used to show the connection between the two graphs?

10 The line graph shows the highest and lowest temperatures each month. Complete the following sentences about the graph by choosing the correct alternative.

1 Proportionally, *both/neither* the lowest possible and highest possible temperatures follow a similar trend and show a peak during the summer months.
2 There is a *strong/large* correlation between the two lines.
3 There appears to be a *limited/significant* correlation between the temperature and the rate of illness.

11 What is the difference between sentences a and b?
a There is no correlation between the two trends.
b There is a negative correlation between the two.

> **Technique**
>
> If you have more than one graphic, identify similarities and trends that might be linked but be clear if they are not. Remember not to make statements based on supposition – you can highlight possible links but demonstrate that this information is not proven by the data. Spend most of the time looking at information given.

Task 2 Word class

1 What do you do to keep fit and healthy?

2 Look at the pictures and name the activities. Do you associate these activities with older or younger people or both? Why?

3 Read the statements below from a website about sporting issues and answer the questions.
   a What is the debate about?
   b What reasons are given in the statements to support and oppose the proposal?

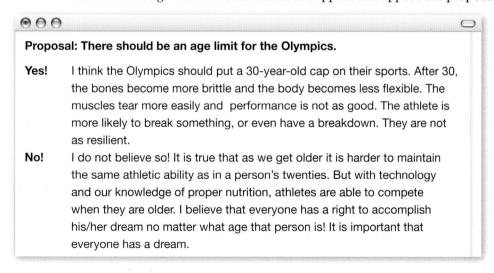

Proposal: There should be an age limit for the Olympics.

Yes! I think the Olympics should put a 30-year-old cap on their sports. After 30, the bones become more brittle and the body becomes less flexible. The muscles tear more easily and performance is not as good. The athlete is more likely to break something, or even have a breakdown. They are not as resilient.

No! I do not believe so! It is true that as we get older it is harder to maintain the same athletic ability as in a person's twenties. But with technology and our knowledge of proper nutrition, athletes are able to compete when they are older. I believe that everyone has a right to accomplish his/her dream no matter what age that person is! It is important that everyone has a dream.

4 Do you agree with the proposal? Why/why not?

5 What motivates a person to compete in sporting events?

6 Some of the words in the table below appear in the website posts in 3. Complete the table with the correct words.

Adjective	Verb	Noun
competitive	compete	*competition*
	✗	athlete
		knowledge
	believe	
	maintain	
	accomplish	
		distinction
	dominate	
significant		
important	✗	

7 Complete the sentences with words from the table in 6. There may be more than one possible answer.

a A/An _____ nature helps a person become more successful in life more generally.

b People who achieve all their goals in life and are skilled or _____ in lots of areas find it more difficult to show sympathy to those who are less successful.

c It is _____ to be _____ and well informed about many areas including art, culture, sport and history.

d To reach the top in the sporting field you probably need to be quite _____ from a young age.

e _____ in your ability to win is key to succeeding.

> **Technique**
>
> Nouns and noun phrases can often make sentences more formal, e.g. *A belief in your own ability* sounds more formal than *Believing in your own ability*.

8 Do you agree or disagree with the statements in 7? Why/why not?

9 Look at the Task 2 question and plan below. How many points are there in the main body of the essay?

> *You should spend about 40 minutes on this task.*
>
> **Some people suggest that sport helps people learn about teamwork but others say it can encourage people to be too competitive. Discuss both views and give your own opinion.**
>
> *Write at least 250 words.*

	Benefit	Drawback
Idea one	Learn how to work with others to succeed. ▷	For some people the only motivation is winning. A
Idea two	Encourages people to be resilient and support each other even when it is hard. B	Teaches people to be aggressive in order to achieve what they want. C
Idea three	People learn about losing as well as winning. E	Don't learn that some aspects of life are not competitive. C

10 Add the following sentences to the correct place in the plan in 9. There is one sentence for each section of the plan.

    a This can lead to people feeling that if they are not first, they have let themselves down and there is no point in making much effort.

    b It isn't unusual for sports to be challenging, so this resilience is important.

    c It is important to understand this to cope better in life.

    d They might have ideas to help win.

    e Knowing this gives us a more rounded attitude to life.

    f Not a healthy approach in general.

> **Technique**
>
> It is important to avoid overgeneralizing. In order to do this, try to include supporting evidence when you make statements.

11 The sentences below contain a main idea and supporting evidence. Complete the sentences using a relative pronoun and the correct form of *to be* or a modal verb.

    a It is significant that for some competitive people the only motivation is winning, ___*which can*___ lead to people feeling they have let themselves down if they don't come first.

    b It is important to learn how to work with other people, _____ have ideas to help with success.

    c A dominant idea is that being competitive encourages people to be resilient, _____ important as sports are often challenging and require people to support each other.

    d Significantly, sport teaches people to gain what they want by being aggressive, _____ not a healthy approach in general.

12 The main idea in each sentence in 11 is signposted with an adjective or related form from 6. Underline each one.

13 Find the errors in the sentences and correct them.

    a Jogging is a sport who you can do with no special equipment.

    b Having a trainer who understand about exercise can help you get fit more quickly.

    c The athlete, won the world championship, has made a great deal of money.

    d His football career ended when he broke his leg that was crucial to his sporting ability.

    e The referee, who we depend to keep the score, is not well today.

    f The games, none of who they won, were well attended.

14 Are the following rules true or false? Why/why not?

    a Defining relative clauses give essential information.

    b Defining relative clauses give additional information, often separated with commas.

    c *That* can be used for people, but only in non-defining relative clauses.

    d The relative pronoun can be missed out if it is a subject relative clause.

    e Any dependent prepositions should be omitted in relative clauses.

    f *None, both* or a number can come before *of which* or *of whom* in a non-defining relative clause.

15 Look at the two examples of a relative clause with a preposition below. Which is more formal and why?

    a The referee, who we depend on to keep the score, is not well today.

    b The referee, on whom we depend to keep the score, is not well today.

16 Rewrite each pair of sentences to make one sentence. Use a relative clause.

    a Many people are interested in the sport. The sport could not be accommodated in a centre big enough to run the competition.

    b The final result was overruled by the referee. Nevertheless, everyone had agreed with the result.

    c The game was watched by 25 000 people. A third of them watched on digital TV.

    d Teenagers generally agree sport is healthy. None of them do much themselves.

    e Many participants in the survey did some kind of physical activity. Twenty-three per cent of the participants went to the gym.

17 Read the conclusion written for the essay plan in 9. Find an example of:

    a a relative clause

    b a signposting noun

> To sum up, I believe that sport has significance in helping people learn about life.
> [1] Although many people, especially those who see more extreme behaviour at football matches, point out the problems that can be caused by extreme fans, [2] such an argument could apply to any activity where participants sometimes behave badly.
> [3] This is not caused by sport in itself. [4] In general I would therefore argue that sport is beneficial to society.

18 Match the sentences/clauses 1–4 in 17 to the functions a–d.

    a restate opinion

    b summarize opposite viewpoint

    c state opinion

    d refute opposite viewpoint

19 Find two phrases in the conclusion in 17 that could be replaced with the expressions in the box.

> in conclusion ■ in the final analysis ■ lastly ■ overall ■ to conclude ■ ultimately

20 Imagine you have written an essay discussing the proposal in 3 on page 65. Write a concluding paragraph using at least one of the expressions in 19. Try to include a relative clause and a signposting word.

> ### Technique
> When you edit your work, look for sentences that provide additional information. These can often be combined into a complex form with the key information using a relative clause.

Practice Test 8

Task 1

You should spend about 20 minutes on this task.

The bar chart shows the number of volunteers in New Zealand who helped in sports organizations in 2010. The pie chart illustrates the number of volunteers doing different types of jobs for that same period. Summarize the information by selecting and reporting the main features, and make comparisons where relevant.

Write at least 150 words.

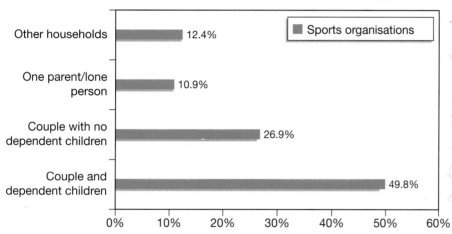

Proportion of volunteers by household type

- Other households — 12.4%
- One parent/lone person — 10.9%
- Couple with no dependent children — 26.9%
- Couple and dependent children — 49.8%

■ Sports organisations

(handwritten annotations:) Amount percentage / structure of family

(handwritten right margin:) The bar chart illustrate the percentage of people volunteering in sports org in N.Z in 2010. This is broken down into categories based of family type / f. structure for example one parent couple with dependent child etc. Whereas the pie chart shows what jobs the volunteering do

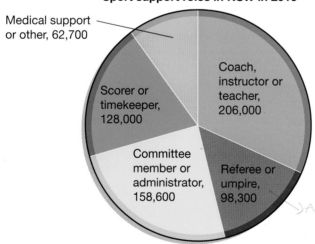

Sport support roles in NSW in 2010

- Medical support or other, 62,700
- Scorer or timekeeper, 128,000
- Coach, instructor or teacher, 206,000
- Committee member or administrator, 158,600
- Referee or umpire, 98,300

(handwritten: Arbitro)

Task 2

You should spend about 40 minutes on this task.

In recent years sports stars have become increasingly famous and wealthy. For some this is a benefit, raising the profile of sports, but for others it is a negative influence. Discuss both views and give your own opinion.

Write at least 250 words.

(handwritten notes at bottom:)
+ makes sport more pop. more people play - healthy, more funding → OXYGEN
+ role models children
- wealth/fame - want to be good at sport just for money
- scandals because of stress pressure   - Ticket prices

Crime
and money

TASK 1 Crime vocabulary
Clarifying meaning
Using articles

TASK 2 Language related to money
Softening and hedging statements
Solutions essay

Task 1 Clarifying meaning

1 Complete the word chain with words from the box. Each word should collocate with the word it links to, e.g. *anti-* collocates with the word in a. Word c collates with words d and e.

> anti- ∎ behaviour ∎ conviction ∎ criminal ∎ hardened
> previous ∎ rate ∎ social

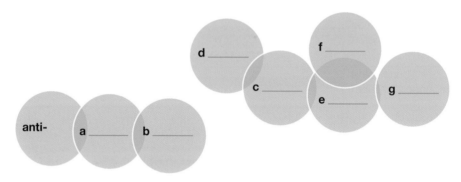

2 Choose the best alternative to complete the sentences.

1 One purpose of punishment is to correct the anti-social behaviour of the
   a offender.
   b witness.

2 Punishment can also be seen as a warning to others and acts as a
   a signal.
   b deterrent.

3 The third reason for punishment is related to revenge, in other words
   a revolt.
   b retribution.

4 Types of punishment vary and there is often a dispute about capital punishment, otherwise known as
   a the death penalty.
   b corporal punishment.

5 Many people are opposed to capital punishment as they think it isn't
   a humane.
   b human.

6 Many believe prison allows the criminal to change and become better, that is
   a rehabilitate
   b feel guilty.

7 Many ex-prisoners go on to live a life free from
   a wrongdeeds.
   b wrongdoing.

8 They give up their previous lifestyle and go on to be
   a law-abiding.
   b law-conforming.

3 Why do you think people commit crimes?

4 What is the purpose of punishment, in your opinion?

5 What do you think the punishment for murder should be?

6 Look at the pie chart and read the model paragraph below. Find 5 factual errors in the paragraph.

Crime
Breakdown of 9.6 million offences based on interviews conducted in 2010/11.

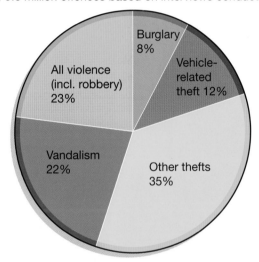

The pie chart illustrates the proportion of different crimes committed in 2011, and includes four different crime categories. In other words it looks at the rates of theft, burglary, vehicle-related crime, violent crime and vandalism. Theft made up the largest proportion at 35 per cent. This was three times as high as the rate for burglary, which was a mere 12 per cent. The lowest proportion of offences related to vehicle theft and this made up only 8 per cent of the total. Combined with vehicle theft, violent crime made up an equivalent proportion to theft in general, standing at 23 per cent on its own. That is to say, when added together they made up a total of 35 per cent. Finally, the second highest proportion of crime was vandalism at 22 per cent.

7 Correct the errors in 6 so that the pie chart is described accurately.

8 Find two phrases in the paragraph in 6 which express clarification.

9 Look at the following phrases, which express clarification. Which are suitable for written and which are suitable for spoken English? Some are suitable for both.
  a By this I mean …
  b To be more precise …
  c What I mean is ….
  d Here I'm referring to …
  e This refers to …

Technique

Read the question several times and think carefully. Ensure you include all the elements required in your answer and answer it fully, or you will lose marks. It is better to spend a bit longer analysing the task and getting this right.

10 Look at the Task 1 question and related sentences below. Complete the sentences with suitable clarification phrases. Use a different phrase each time.

You should spend about 20 minutes on this task.

The graph shows the number of prisoners in the UK between 2005 and 2009. Summarize the information by selecting and reporting the main features, and make comparisons where relevant.

Write at least 150 words.

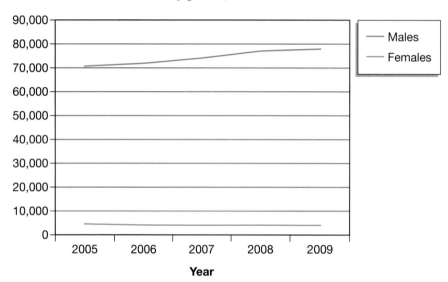

Prison population including foreign nationals by gender, 2005–2009

a The number of male prisoners consistently outstrips the number of women, _____ there are far more men than women in prison.

b Women prisoners remain consistently low throughout the period, or _____ , the proportion of women remained at approximately 4 000 or 5 000 between 2005 and 2009.

c The number of men peaked towards the end of the period. _____ , there were just under 80 000 male prisoners in 2009.

11 Look back at the model paragraph in 6. Underline the following nouns or noun phrases.
  a theft
  b violent crime
  c for burglary
  d lowest proportion
  e equivalent proportion
  f second highest

12 Does each noun in 11 have an article (*a/an/the*) or no article?

13 Match the sentences 1–5 to the rules a–e.
1 Violent crime is too high.
2 The violent crime he committed was the second he was convicted of doing.
3 Knowledge about the causes of crime needs further development.
4 The young are often accused of petty crime.
5 *The Times* reported new research on the effects of prison.

a definite article used for specific items such as newspapers, mountain ranges, media, musical instruments and so on; abstract and uncountable nouns given no article
b abstract and uncountable nouns often have no article
c uncountable nouns are used with the definite article when referred to as a group, e.g. *the rich, the unemployed*
d uncountable nouns have no article except when qualified, e.g. in phrases using *of*: *crime/the causes of crime*
e definite article used with superlatives and numbers, e.g. *the first, the last, the longest*

14 Decide if each gap needs an article or no article. Then complete the sentences.

a People have long used _____ punishment to try and stop

_____ sort of crime that is easily solved with good deterrents.

b _____ punishment can also be seen as _____ revenge,

in other words as _____ kind of _____ retribution for

_____ victims who were damaged by _____ crime.

c _____ most obvious _____ punishment for more serious

_____ crime is _____ prison.

d Other types of _____ punishment include _____ fines and

work in the community, although there is often _____ argument about

_____ capital punishment or _____ death penalty.

e Many people are opposed to _____ fines as they think these don't punish

_____ criminal enough.

Technique

Articles can be complex as there are so many exceptions. Reading a lot will improve your sense of where and when not to use them.

Task 2 Softening and hedging statements

1 Complete the table by putting words and phrases from the box in the correct category.

> affluent ▪ broke ▪ cash ▪ coins ▪ destitute ▪ dough ▪ funding ▪ impoverished
> making ends meet ▪ prosperous ▪ wealthy ▪ well off

money	rich	poor

2 Which words in 1 are formal and which are informal?

3 Do you think that money is often the cause of crime? In what ways?

4 How much are you motivated by money?

5 Read about the history of money and answer the questions.
   a Where was the first metal money used? *China*
   b How were coins originally valued? *By weight*
   c What led to coins being used more widely?

Bartering was the original form of money, as people in the ancient world exchanged food or animals to get what they wanted. The Chinese were the first to use metal money made from bronze or copper, although they also used 'tool' money such as spades in exchanges. They paved the way for an age in which people were obsessed by coins, it seems.
In 500 BC in Lydia, now part of Turkey, coins made partly from gold were used. These were all irregular in shape and historians believe their value was possibly established by weight rather than size. Similar coinage systems then built up in Greece and Egypt and due to the ease with which they could be transported, the coins were eventually carried around, their value written on the surface rather than being determined by weighing.

6 Decide if the following statements are facts or the opinion of the writer of the text in 5.

  1 Money has always been a part of human life in one form or another. F
  2 It is important to have ways of trading goods so that we can get what we need. F
  3 Use of coins was the beginning of a monetary age in which coins became a key motivation for people. O
  4 Money has been a dominating force ever since it was first invented. O
  5 Money proved a convenient way to continue a process begun with bartering. F

> **Technique**
> Think carefully about how you want to present information. Most writers do not write *I think* or similar expressions. They use other devices to indicate opinion rather than fact. You should try to use a range of these to vary your writing and to make it sound balanced rather than one-sided.

7 Match the sentences a and b with two of the sentences in 6. How do they differ?

  a It seems that use of coins was the beginning of a monetary age in which coins became a key motivation for people.
  b It is probable that money has been a dominating force ever since it was first invented.

8 The sentences below contain softening or 'hedging' language. Underline the words which soften each sentence.

  a It appears that money brings out the worst in people.
  b Money possibly encourages people to work harder than they otherwise would.
  c There is a tendency for people to weaken their moral position if they think they can make a profit.
  d Occasionally we realize the extent to which materialism controls our life nowadays.

> **Technique**
> It is important to show that you understand different viewpoints are possible. Hedging – softening language – demonstrates this and works well in academic writing.

9 Match the words and phrases you underlined in 8 with 1–4.

  1 a verb form
  2 a frequency adverb form
  3 a fixed expression
  4 a probability adverb

10 Match the words and phrases a–d with 1–4 in 9.

  a rarely
  b maybe
  c It is claimed that
  d It seems that

11 The following statements are overgeneralized or too direct. Soften them using expressions from 8–10.

  a The banks have too much power. It seems that
  b People need to get support to understand about finances.
  c Materialistic attitudes are very unhealthy. It seems that
  d There would be less crime in the world if we didn't have systems of money.
  e If you are only motivated by money, you won't be happy. probably

> **Technique**
> Remember that it is important to be clear about your position or opinion when answering the Task 2 question. You can demonstrate it all the way through the essay.

12 Look at the Task 2 question below. What kind of essay is this and what structure will your answer usually have?

> *You should spend about 40 minutes on this task.*
>
> **Some people find it difficult to manage their money. How could the government help prevent debt problems and support such people?**
>
> *Write at least 250 words.*

13 Think of 3 or 4 possible solutions to the problem.

14 Add the ideas 1–3 to the correct place in the plan below. Are any the same as your ideas?

1 Most important idea – educate people to understand how to manage money. Government should provide lessons in school. Advantage – people will be much more competent. Drawback – would take up time, e.g. in schools time needed for other things.

2 Finally, banks and shops shouldn't lend to people who don't have enough money. Advantage – people don't have opportunity for debt. Drawback – could cause hardship if people desperately need credit.

3 Also, could be advisory centres for free advice. Advantage – would help people before their problems became serious. Disadvantage – expensive to run.

Introduction	Many people have money problems. Not due to poverty. Due to bad money management. Therefore knowing what to do with money important.
Solution 1 – benefit and drawback	**a** Most important idea – educate people to understand how manage money. 1 Government should provide lessons in school. Advantage – people will be much more competent. Drawback – would take up time, eg. in schools time needed for other things
Solution 2 – benefit and drawback	**b** Also could be advisory centres for free advice. Advantage – would help people 3 before their problems became serious. Disadvantage – expensive to run
Solution 3 – benefit and drawback	**c** Finally, banks and shops shouldn't lend to people who don't have enough money. 2 Advantage – people don't have opportunity for debt. Drawback – could cause hardship if people desperately need credit.
Conclusion	All these solutions help. But the first most important as lets people learn and look after their own finances better.

15 Write out one or more of the paragraphs using the **plan in 14** to help you. Include softening phrases.

> ### Technique
> Read through your paragraphs checking for spelling, variety of expressions, vocabulary and grammar. Get into the habit of doing this regularly and it will be easier when you do the exam.

Practice Test 9

Task 1

You should spend about 20 minutes on this task. gender   type of crime

The bar chart shows the number of male and female people arrested by type of offence (crime). Summarize the information by selecting and reporting the main features, and make comparisons where relevant.

Write at least 150 words.

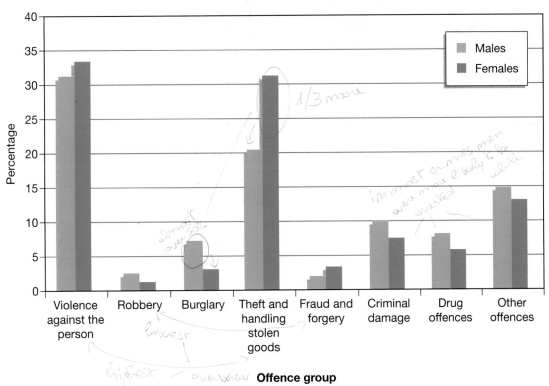

Proportion of male and female arrests by offence type, 2008/09

1/3 more

in most crimes men
were more likely to be
arrested

almost
over 30%

lowest

highest   overview

Task 2

You should spend about 40 minutes on this task.

How can the government make sure that people save enough money to live on when they are old?

Write at least 250 words.

TASK 1   The bar chart gives information on the numbers of/percentage of people/men & women arrested for various crimes in 2008/09. This information is presented as a % divided by gender & type of crime

10 Language
and culture

UNIT AIMS

TASK 1 Synonyms
Understanding data information
Review of linkers

TASK 2 Essay types
Typical errors
Editing your work

Task 1 Synonyms

1 Complete the advice about taking a writing exam with words from the box.

> address ■ analysing ■ ensure ■ generalize ■ key ■ miss out ■ paraphrase
> predictable ■ range ■ state

When taking a writing exam such as IELTS, [1] .... that you know the typical topics which might arise. These can be fairly [2] .... but even so, be careful to read the question carefully. You should be sure to [3] .... every part of the question; many people either [4] .... too much or [5] .... some parts. Don't write out the question. Try to [6] .... it instead.

Once you have finished [7] .... the question, write a plan. Include [8] .... points and supporting evidence. If appropriate, make sure you [9] .... your viewpoint clearly and also use a wide [10] .... of language including interesting vocabulary and grammar. And don't forget a strong introduction and conclusion.

2 In each pair of words below, only one is a viable synonym for 1–10 in 1. Circle the correct words.

1 check/assume
2 foreseeable/unavoidable
3 arrange/tackle
4 make sweeping statements/make stipulations
5 fail/omit

6 translate/rephrase
7 inspecting/evaluating
8 significant/chief
9 testify/express
10 selection/scale

3 At what age did you begin learning English? Do you think there is there an age when you can learn more easily?

4 Read the text below. What does it tell you about the best age for language learning? Does it suggest a correlation between language learning and age?

> Researchers constantly disagree about age and the ability to learn language. One theory is that there is a 'critical period' and if you try to learn after this period it is more difficult. Others disagree and believe it is other factors that make it more difficult. One study from 1989 investigated how quickly immigrants learnt a language and found that those who began youngest were able to learn the most.

5 Read the text below about a study of language learning. Complete the bar chart with information from the text. First label the columns 1–4. Then draw the bars.

The bar chart illustrates the results of an English test taken by four groups of immigrants, all of whom arrived in the USA when they were different ages. The groups were made up of those who arrived in the USA between ages 3 and 7, those aged 8 to 10, a third group covering ages 11 to 15 and finally those who emigrated after the age of 17.

Overall, it is evident that the immigrants who were younger at their time of arrival achieved a much greater level of proficiency in the language. Those who were 3 to 7 when they emigrated scored an average of 98 per cent in the test, the highest overall outcome. However, this level of proficiency dropped rapidly for those who arrived age 17 or over; the oldest group achieved an average score

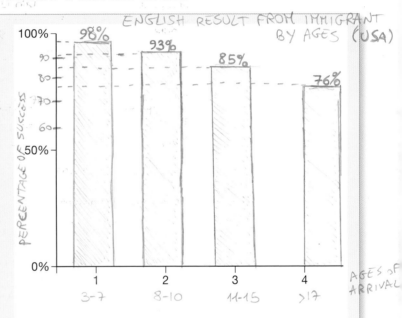

of 76 per cent, which is the lowest proportion. This trend is further supported by the scores of the other age groups; those who arrived aged 8 to 10 also did better than those arriving aged 11 to 15, achieving 93 per cent and 85 per cent respectively.

In conclusion, we can see that the bar chart demonstrates a consistent decrease in the proficiency levels of immigrants according to their age on arrival. It seems the younger they arrive, the quicker they are likely to learn English to a proficient degree.

Technique

If you have written a good essay, a reader should be able to draw a rough graph of the information. If they can't, you haven't written clearly enough.

6 What are the highest and lowest points described in the text in 5?

7 Put the underlined words from the text in 5 in the correct place in the table below.
Then add the words from the box to the table.

> although ■ as ■ but ■ despite ■ due to ■ for example ■ for instance ■ firstly ■ furthermore
> hence ■ in addition to ■ in order to ■ moreover ■ nevertheless ■ next ■ on the other hand
> since ■ so ■ so as to ■ so long as ■ subsequently ■ such as ■ therefore ■ to ■ unless
> whereas ■ while

Ordering ideas	Additions	Contrast	Concession (softene--)
Firstly Next Subsequently Finally Lastly	In addition to Furthermore Moreover Also	Whereas While On the other hand But	Despite Nevertheless Unless However Although So long as
Showing reason	**Showing result**	**Showing purpose**	**Exemplification**
Due to As Since As a result of the tree blew down due to/as/... there was a storm	Therefore Hence So There was a storm so/ therefore /hence the tree blew down	So as to To In order to	For example For instance Such as

8 Complete the sentences with an appropriate linking word or expression. More
than one answer may be possible.

a It is hard to learn a new language. _However_, many people make the
effort.

b Travelling is an excellent way to meet new people _but_ you have
to get out of the hotel to do this.

c _Since_ he wants to study science, he is taking biology, chemistry
and physics at school.

d The business plan is going well. _Firstly_ they did a lot of research
and then they got in the right team to work on it and finally they found some
excellent investors.

e The population has risen dramatically and _as a result_ there is pressure on
housing.

f _Despite_ learning various sports, the children said they hadn't got much
exercise.

g _In addition to_ deforestation, global warming is also caused by air and water
pollution and industrial and farming practices.

h The olives are pressed _in order to_ make olive oil.

i You can study a number of courses _such as_ art or interior design.

j The exam was tough _despite_ he passed with flying colours.

> **Technique**
>
> It is important to use a
> good range of linking
> expressions but don't
> use too many or it will
> sound very unnatural.
> Change the linkers and
> use them to help the
> flow of the essay, but
> don't overdo it and check
> that punctuation is used
> correctly.

Task 2 Typical errors

1 Think of answers for the questions below.

   a How easy is it to learn a language?
   b Which languages are spoken most in the world?
   c How many languages are endangered?
   d Are there any artificial languages?
   e What is the best way to learn a language?

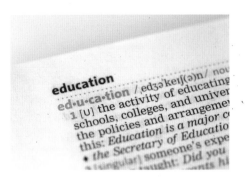

2 Match the answers 1–5 with the questions a–e in 1.

   1 It is claimed that 2 500 languages are in danger of disappearing. Some have less than 1 000 speakers.

   2 This varies from person to person – no single way has been found. If you understand your learning style, you can identify the way that works best for you.

   3 The most spoken languages are Mandarin Chinese and English. Spanish is the third most common language.

   4 It is easier to learn a language that is similar to your own. Therefore, a Polish speaker will find Slavic languages easier to learn than others.

   5 Around 200 artificial languages have been invented since the 17th century. The best known is Esperanto with 2 million speakers.

Technique

When we write in English we usually put the complex information at the end of the sentence. But in an academic essay we sometimes order the information differently. We use

a nominalization (creating nouns).
b participle clauses.
c 'cleft' sentences (*It is … who …* or *It was … that …*).

---

3 Read the example and match sentences 1–3 with a technique a–c from the box above.

   People who can speak another language fluently earn, on average, approximately 8 per cent more than people who don't.
   1 It is speaking another language that can increase our wages by approximately 8 per cent.
   2 Bilingualism can increase our wages by 8 per cent.
   3 Speaking another language fluently allows us to earn approximately 8 per cent more.

4 Rewrite the sentences in 2 using one of the three techniques from the box.

5 Look at the following essay questions. Match a question with an essay type in the table a–d.

   1 Learning a second language is often seen as important nowadays but many people fail to do so. What measures would help more people to learn?

   2 All schoolchildren should learn another language whether they would like to or not. Is this realistic? Give reasons for your answers and include any relevant examples from your own knowledge or experience.

   3 Some people believe that travel is beneficial while others argue that increased travel and globalization is destroying local cultures. Discuss both viewpoints and give your own opinion.

   4 Taking a year to travel after university is of great benefit to young people. To what extent do you agree?

a Theory-based essay	2
b Contrasting viewpoints essay	3
c Evaluation and opinion essay	4
d Problem-solving essay	1

6 Match the plans 1–4 to the question types a–d in 5.

Plan 1

- introduce topic   C
- state opinion
- justify opinion
- summarize

Plan 2

- idea or theory   A
- my reason and supporting evidence
- further reason and supporting evidence
- conclusion

Plan 3   B

- topic introduced
- idea 1: benefits and drawbacks
- idea 2: benefits and drawbacks
- conclusion and final opinion

Plan 4   D

- problem introduced
- solution 1: advantages and disadvantages
- solution 2: advantages and disadvantages
- conclusion

> **Technique**
>
> Make sure you have fully analysed the question and decided on the overall pattern of your essay. This will help you at the writing stage and give a good flow to the essay.

7 Read the first part of two different essays quickly. Which question from 5 does each answer?

> a This idea is something I agree with. I think they should definitely travel because it is good to broaden your mind and ideas. Travel does this. You can also learn a language from it. An example is one friend of mine who travelled and when she returned home she had a more positive outlook and ideas about the world. It is good for this reason. It gives you a chance to experiment and find out about yourself. This will also make you more understanding of the people and cultures around you.

> b It is true to say that, even though the world is becoming increasingly globalized and international communication is important, people are still not learning a second language, unfortunately. Also, they don't learn enough about other cultures. Moreover, they don't think it is a disadvantage that they don't speak another language. There are a variety of solutions that might help with this problem.

8 Which problems can you see in the paragraphs in 7? Complete the checklist of the most common problems. Tick the boxes on the right.

	a	b
1 no clear introduction setting up the ideas		
2 unclear planning – no central idea in each paragraph		
3 basic sentences which lack variety		
4 repetition of vocabulary		
5 lack of cohesion or overuse of linkers		
6 lack of referencing		
7 poor grammar		
8 poor spelling		
9 unclear viewpoint or overgeneralized statements		
10 no clear conclusion		

9 There are two key ideas in the first essay extract: travel can broaden the mind and helps people learn about themselves; it also allows people to learn another language and learn about each other. Rewrite the paragraph following the points below.

a Introduce your ideas clearly.
b State the first idea and support it with evidence.
c State the second idea and support it with evidence.
d Include some reference words and try to avoid repetition.

10 Rewrite the second essay extract by removing the excess linking words.

11 Each of the following sentences has a typical spelling or grammar error. Find and correct the errors.

a The number of people learning Chinese are increasing.
b Many people had started to learn this to increase their employment prospects.
c A culture is constantly changing as people travel the globe.
d Communications is important in maintaining good relations between countries.
e Due to this it is easier to learn a language
f There is an increase in intercultural relationships and marriage of a foreigner.
g The people which have travelled are more open-minded.
h Being well-travelling is a positive characteristic.

> **Technique**
> When you write your essays, allow five minutes at the end to check your work. Do this systematically. Think about content, organization and flow, if your ideas are clearly presented, if there is a strong introduction and conclusion, and check for grammar and spelling.

12 Match the types of error 1–8 with the sentences in 11.

1 incomplete sentences
2 word form
3 agreement between subject and verb
4 countable and uncountable nouns
5 relative clauses
6 articles
7 tense
8 prepositions

13 Read an extract from the essay about travelling after university. Find and correct the errors.

Travel can be very benefit to the young people in many ways and therefore gap years, which is students travel abroad for a time before embarking upon a career, can be very useful for people as they grow up. I would therefore maintain that travelling was a positive experience for young people.

First, travelling allows people to broaden their minds to learning about an unknown culture. And by spending time abroad the person will experienced new and unique events. They can learn a great deal about the world around them. In general this type of experience also helps people to develop their own personality. Because they begin to carve out their own opinions from a wider perspective.

Also second, they can find a lot about the rest of the world such as learning another language and meeting new people. This will make them more richer as a person when they eventually settle down and start to working. This must be a big advantag and give them a good start to working life.

Finally they will have been learning responsibility and autonomousness because of their experience.

Therefore, for these reasons, all in all I agree that people should try to travel after their studies finish.

Practice Test 10

Task 1

You should spend about 20 minutes on this task.

im Dec 2001

The pie chart shows the number of people who were using different languages online. The table shows the average number of people online each year. Summarize the information by selecting and reporting the main features, and make comparisons where relevant.

Write at least 150 words.

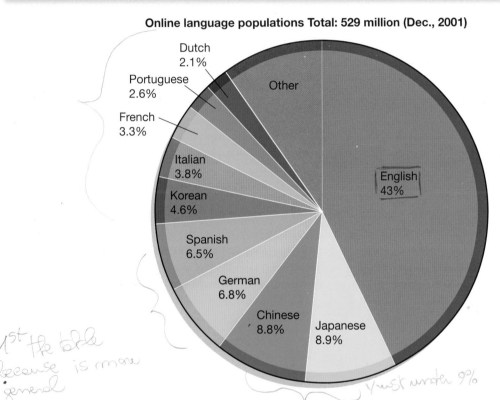

Online language populations Total: 529 million (Dec., 2001)

Dutch 2.1%
Portuguese 2.6%
French 3.3%
Italian 3.8%
Korean 4.6%
Spanish 6.5%
German 6.8%
Chinese 8.8%
Japanese 8.9%
Other
English 43%

1st the table because is more general

must write 9%

Date	Number in millions	% of world population
August 2001	513	8.4
August 2000	368	60
August 1999	195	4.6
September 1998	147	3.6
November 1997	76	1.8

still small percentage *almost doubled*
overall increase
double
de. t suggest that is doubling almost every year

Task 2

You should spend about 40 minutes on this task.

Nowadays many countries have very cosmopolitan cities with people from all over the world. How can the government ensure that all these people can live together harmoniously?

Write at least 250 words.

Sample
answers

The publishers stress that these are not official grades and are for guidance only. There is no guarantee that these answers would obtain these grades in the test.

Practice Test 1

Task 1

The graph illustrate the amount of money earned per week by graduates of different age groups who are working. It consider graduates who have a degree or a higher degree as well as those with other qualifications.

In general, people with other types of qualification earn the most at all ages except in the oldest age group. In contrast, those with first degrees mainly earn the least throughout.

All three types of graduate see a dramatic rise in wages between ages 21 to 25 and 36 to 45. The wages of graduates with first and higher degrees reach a high point at ages 41 to 45 whereas the wages of those with other qualifications reach their maximum slightly earlier, hitting a peak for those aged 36 to 40. Wages for people with other types of qualification then gradually decrease to £700 per week and stay at that level. But income for people with a higher degree rise quite sharply to reach a highest point for 56 to 60 year olds. *(170 words)*

Grade: 5

Comment: This answer is reasonably well structured and gives a summary of the graph after the introduction. It covers all the main information and trends. The vocabulary and grammar is not bad although there are some errors all the way through. However, the biggest weakness is that it does not give evidence or detail to support the description of the trends.

Task 2

Nowadays some schools offer work experience in addition to normal study, giving students the chance to gain some insight into real working situations while also having more traditional academic qualifications. Some employers have recently suggested that young people can graduate from school or university lacking the necessary tools to survive in the world of employ.

In my opinion, whilst it is essential that young people gain qualifications, it is also important that they develop a conscious of what will be expected from them in a job. For this reason I think it is a good sense for teenagers to make some work experience as part of their education.

Of course, having qualifications will always be assets but only if the young person is also able to adept quickly to the expectations of their employer. There is no benefit in being exceptionally qualified if you don't know what to do on a daily life. By doing work experience, even if it is only making the coffee or photocopies, young people will quickly learn work based skills such as time management and ability for dealing with people of all ages.

Furthermore, having work experience demonstrates diligence in a real working context, making the student more employable. Not only does it give them a valuable advantage, it also offers them insight too; they are able to see what certain types of job entail at close range which will enable them to make an informed choice about their plans for the future.

Of course there are some small drawbacks to the idea of work experience; students might get distracted by work and not study. However this is outweighed by the gains made by gaining the experience. Overall it is therefore a good idea for students to do some kind of work experience. *(278 words)*

Grade: 7

Comment: This answer has a key idea for each paragraph and is logically organized. The writer has given his/her opinion very clearly and all the ideas support the main opinion. The grammar is good and the sentences generally link together. However, there are some errors with vocabulary which reduce the positive impact of the writing.

Practice Test 2

Task 1

The table provides information about the sales rates of five major types of mobile phone from 2006 to 2012.

There are three clear trends visible in the data. Firstly, two phone brands, Samsung and Apple, demonstrated a consistent rise in sales during the six-year period, Samsung finishing with the highest level of sales overall at 396.5 million in 2012. While Apple made the lowest number of sales at the start, with a mere 2.3 million in 2007, this soared to just under 136 million by the end of the period, paralleling the growth of Samsung's sales and putting Apple in third highest position.

Nokia had a higher number of sales than Apple at the finish with a total of 335 million; however this was a marked drop from a previous high of 475 million in 2008. Nokia's sales were slightly erratic in general, rising rapidly from 2006 to 2008 before dropping in 2009, then repeating the cycle by improving to 463 million in 2010 before slipping downwards to its final result in 2012.

Finally two other brands, Motorola and Ericsson, followed a more persistently downward pattern. Both suffered the lowest number of sales overall, achieving only 28 million sales each in 2012. Ericsson's sales dropped rapidly from the highest point of 102 million in 2007 before levelling out and decreasing far less dramatically from 2010 where they were at 42 million.

Overall two brands improved their sales, two brands showed dramatic drops and one brand had a mixed performance with a negative trend at the end of the period. *(257 words)*

Grade: 9

Comment: This is a good answer with an organized structure and lots of supporting detail. The vocabulary is used accurately and there are no spelling or grammar errors. There is a summary of the information included at the end. However, it is a long answer and this could impact on the performance of the candidate when answering Task 2.

Task 2

The internet is an important part of life in modern times. It has changed our lives in many ways and made it easier to do many things. In my opinion I agree with this. I will first look at some ideas why and then some benefits.

Internet has made shopping much easier. Before we had to go to a supermarket or shopping centre to buy things. Now we can use the internet. If I want something I can order online and it will come to me and it doesn't matter whether the shop is in the same place or not. It is an advantage like travelling.

Internet means we can find tickets to places easily. We can book our own plane ticket and even choose the place we sit. We don't have to do check in at the airport. It is easy to find the information because we can look it up on the internet. In the past people had to go to a library or information centre and it wasn't so easy and quick to find what they wanted.

Also we can communicate quickly with internet. We can use email instead of letters and we can use Skype or other communication methods instead of phoning which can be expensive or difficult. We can find everything more easily: for example if we want to find a house to rent or hire a car.

Without the internet life is more inconvenient. Normal activities take much longer to do and we can't find what we need as easily. I agree that the internet made life more convenient. *(265 words)*

Sample answers

Grade: 5

Comment: The writer states an opinion clearly and the ideas in the essay relate well to the question. However, they are not well organized; paragraph two is about shopping but paragraphs three and four mention travel, finding information, communication then finding things again. Each paragraph should have a clear central idea, not a mixture. Vocabulary and grammar is generally well managed, but rather basic, and the sentences are not linked very well.

Practice Test 3

Task 1

The flow chart demonstrates the effects of tourists in the countryside and the issues that are caused by them walking in the countryside. When tourists walk there the number of people stepping in the same places causes a problem. This is because a lot of people walk on the same ground which means they damage the vegetation underfoot. At the same time the soil they stand on gets compacted. As the vegetation is damaged, the plants that are left get weaker. The weaker plants don't grow much and they don't reproduce. This means the amount of vegetation and growth decreases. Also the hardened soil which is compacted when people walk over it doesn't have the normal amounts of air and water creating a less healthy soil. The soil erodes more quickly and water runs off the land as a result. This also leads to less growth. Therefore the damage to the vegetation and the compacted soil both lead to poor soil and erosion. *(163 words)*

Grade: 6

Comment: The answer is comprehensive but it adds in information which is not actually shown in the diagram, e.g. numbers of tourists causing greater damage. These facts may be true but the task requires the writer to describe the information given and not make deductions and guesses. The vocabulary and grammar is accurate and all the information is covered, which is a good feature. However, the flow of the text isn't strong and there is a fair amount of repetition.

Task 2

The 'gap year' is now common phenomenon, with young graduates travelling to distant places before they settle down on their first long term job. Such travels can be seen as hugely beneficial, a way of developing a person's interest and understanding of the world, or alternatively viewed as time spent irresponsibly. Although I have some sympathy with the latter view, ultimately I believe that gap year can be very rewarding.

For many people, a student should begin work as soon as university is finished since a gap year is simply an extendable, self-indulgent holiday. They claim that 'gappers' end up in holiday resorts and do not even see much culture. While there is probably some truth in this, any kind of travel is an important experience in expanding a person's world view. Furthermore, although some people may spend part of that time in resorts, many more do voluntary work or backpack and gain a huge amount from the experience.

Similarly, people critic gap years on basis that the person is wasting money instead of earning it. But many graduates would not find work immediately. In fact 'gappers' often work while they travel, gaining world and work experience which will help them find employment on their return.

Another argument against the gap year is that it takes up time better used beginning a career. However, most people will spend another 40 years or more doing exactly this. Moreover it becomes more and more problematic to take time off as we get older. So the time after university is ideal to learn about the world and gain an experience outside our normal nine to five existence.

Finally while some people see a gap year as unproductive, it should be remembered that a great deal can be achieved in that time; students come back home having done charity or learnt a language in a different country.

In summary, whilst it is true that some people may spend a year on a beach wasting time and money, many more people will find out a great deal about the world around them and themselves during a gap year and it is therefore a beneficial experience. *(360 words)*

Grade: 8

Comment: The arguments in this answer are clear and well developed. They are ordered logically and each paragraph is clear, with a key point made sensibly. The grammar shows lots of different structures and these are mostly very accurate. The vocabulary is effective and demonstrates an ability to use quite colloquial phrases. There are some errors in vocabulary and grammar but these are quite minor and don't follow a pattern.

Practice Test 4

Task 1

The graph shows the number of visitors to a variety of art galleries in 2011. These included the Louvre in France, the Metropolitan Museum in the USA, the British Museum in the UK, the National Museum of Korea, the Museo del Prado in Spain and the State Hermitage in Russia.

In 2011 the Louvre had just under 9 million visitors and this was the highest number of visitors. The Metropolitan Museum had 6 million visitors. The British Museum had just under 6 million. Next was the Museum of Korea which had just over 3 million visitors. The Museo del Prado had 3 million visitors and the State Hermitage had slightly below 3 million.

So the museum with the most visitors was the Louvre and the museum with the least was the State Hermitage museum. *(119 words)*

Grade: 5

Comment: The grammar and structure of this answer is good and there are very few errors. Vocabulary is used accurately although there isn't much variety. The biggest issue is that the answer is under-length. The first sentence is copied from the rubric so doesn't count. One of the reasons the answer is under-length is because the writer does not really make comparisons. The number of visitors to each museum is outlined accurately but except for the last sentence, there is very little comparison.

Task 2

Television is a part of everyday life and most children watch programmes regularly. Many people agree that children if they watch too much television it can be a bad influence and we need to control the way children watch TV to make sure it is not harming.

Firstly, parents should control to the type of programmes that children watch. If they check that the programmes chosen are appropriate ones, TV can be educational. For example, children can learn about the world, learn new words and learn interesting facts. Even fun programmes can teach many things to young people. But this is only possible if the adults check they are not watching inappropriately, e.g. violent films.

Secondly I think TV companies should not show programmes early in the day that would be bad for young people. There should be some protection so that during the afternoon and the evening only suitable programmes are available. This is another protection for the life of children.

In addition, it is important to limit the amount of time spent watching television. If children spend too much on one thing it won't be healthy. TV should be part of a whole range of activities for children. If children do sports, have other hobbies and go out with their friends then TV is a nice relaxing activity for them. It can be a positive influence.

Finally TV can be good in help children to make friends. Most kids watch TV so it give them something to talk about. If they both like a similar cartoon or children's programme, they will be able to discuss it and find something in common.

Therefore, television can be a very positive influence for children. If parents control what the children watch and the type of programmes, television can be a good part of their lives. *(303 words)*

Sample answers

Grade: 6

Comment: The essay is organized into clear paragraphs and completes the task. The ideas are presented in logical order and some linking between sentences and between paragraphs is included. The vocabulary is generally chosen appropriately although there are a few errors and it could be more sophisticated. Grammar follows a similar pattern.

Practice Test 5

Task 1

The line graph indicates the life expectancy of people living in Asian regions starting 1950 up until 2300. Most striking about the graph is trends are all upwards; in most areas of Asia life expectancy more than doubles from average of 40–50 years old in 1950 to expected 90–100 years old in 2300.

The initial rose was steep in each case, especially between 1950 and 2000, the trends have gradually slowed since 2000. They are set to continue rise but at a much slower rate.

The Eastern Asian region offers the longest life expectancy for all the periods shown. In 1950 it was higher than all the other regions at an approximate age of 54 years and it is predicted to peak at a likely 103 or 104 years by 2300.

South-central Asia generally has the lowest life expectancy throughout beginning under 40 years old and predicted to reach just under 90 years old. This trend is closely matched by India which follows almost exactly the same pattern, reaching a year or so higher than South-central Asia, except in the years between 2030 and 2050, where India set to be a year or so behind. *(198 words)*

Grade: 7

Comment: The vocabulary in the answer is strong with some good collocations and natural use of language. A summary is included at the beginning. All the key information is included though the amount of data given as evidence could be higher, especially at the start. There is a good range of grammar but some errors with the word forms and sentence structures.

Task 2

Major cities around the world are beset by a similar problem: traffic congestion. From Shanghai to New York, key cities in most developing or developed countries are tackling congested roads and all the negative consequences that this brings. Finding answers is an ongoing issue.

One key solution for the problem is public transport. In many places this is not convenient and too expensive which means that people still prefer to take their own cars rather than travel by bus, train or underground. Reducing the cost of public transport and checking that it works smoothly, for example by ensuring that buses link to key train stations and run late enough each day, will entice people back onto public transport systems.

Ensuring that this transport has proper staffing, in other words have ticket inspectors and staff at stations, will also help as people will feel safer. This would, for example, allow women travelling alone late at night to still feel secure.

Another way to persuade people to leave their cars at home is by increasing taxes on driving. Charging tax on parking and petrol could bring in more revenue to fund better roads or support other types of transport. For example, higher road tax could fund cycling paths within cities.

However, making travel by private car more difficult is only viable if reliable and affordable alternatives are in place. Another measure which could help is to develop more 'park and ride' schemes where people can park free at the edge of the city and catch a bus in to the centre. There should also be more cycle paths available.

By having better alternatives in place and making them more attractive than using private cars, it may be possible to reduce the increasing problems with traffic congestion that modern cities face. *(301 words)*

Grade: 9

Comment: The essay is well organized and detailed, with all arguments extensive and clear. Grammar, vocabulary and spelling are accurate throughout.

Practice Test 6

Task 1

The diagram shows how shellfish are labelled and packaged before they go to different markets around the world. There are three stages involved: monitoring, labelling and processing.

In the first stage, as the shellfish are caught, a GPS system is used to monitor the fishing boats. Each boat has a location device on it which means a satellite can track and monitor it. This allows the boats to be monitored. When the fishing boat catches any shellfish the location is sent back to the monitoring system so there is a link between the catch and the location.

In the second stage, a barcode label is produced using the location information collected by satellite. These barcodes are then sent to a processing plant along with the shellfish. As the shellfish are processed for market they are also labelled with the correct barcode. The barcodes show where the fish originated. In the final stage of the process, the labelled shellfish are sent to markets in different places.

In conclusion the satellite system is used to track fishing boats and to make sure that the fish are labelled with the place they originated. *(190 words)*

Grade: 8

Comment: The process is clearly and accurately described with each stage covered. There is a summary outlining the different stages. The grammar and vocabulary are appropriate for the task. The spelling is accurate throughout and the sentences are linked fluently and logically overall. The only drawback is that there is some repetition of vocabulary; use of pronouns and referencing devices would have avoided this and made it a smoother read.

Task 2

In some countries, food shortage leading to famine and starving cause serious problems. But in many developed nations the opposite is true: food is easily available but an increasing number of people have issues in obesity and unhealthy nutrition. They have long-term health problems because of high levels of fat and salt intake and they don't eat enough fresh fruit and vegetables.

One suggestion often made is that a tax on fast food would reduce the problem. This may help to reduce the number of people who buy regularly high fat, high salt take away food and also unhealthy fast foods sold in the supermarkets. Many people are inclined to buy this type of food as is often cheap and on special offer. If supermarkets and cafes had to include tax the benefit of the low price would be less. On the other hand, poor people often rely on these kinds of cheap deals to feed their families. Some people may find it very hard to survive if foods become a lot more expensive and this would be unfair on them.

Adding tax to fast foods would work much better if also governments put in some measures to reduct the cost of fruit, vegetables and healthy foods. They could create some laws to ensure that healthier foods were almost always the cheapest options and people could buy them easily whatever their social level. Of course may be difficult for farmers who could lose income. But it would be better for the health of nations.

Another step that could be taken is offer more education at school so that children learn how to cook cheap, healthy foods. Many people buy ready-made meals and take away because they are not confident about cooking. If they learnt doing this better they may choose healthier meals. The only difficulty with this is that life is so busy nowadays people often don't have time and buy fast food because it is quick.

In conclusion, it seems to me that taxing fast food is a good idea but only if it is combined with some other solutions such as making healthy options cheaper and educating people about eating well. *(361 words)*

Grade: 7

Comment: The answer has a good structure with an evaluation of the suggested solution and some alternative solutions also considered. Ideas are all well developed and presented in a logical order. There is a good level of vocabulary but with occasional errors in form. Grammar is mostly solid with some complex sentences included. The basic grammar is mostly OK and it is easy to understand the central point of each paragraph.

Practice Test 7

Task 1

The bar chart offers detailed information about the number of people who had died in injuries at work in New Zealand between dates 1992 and 2010.

Overall the difference in total fatalities each year was not significant. The lowest number of deaths occurred in 2009 with 4,551 fatalities in total; this had been in contrast to 1994 which had the highest total at 6,632.

However there were no clear or significant trends as the total numbers mainly fluctueted across the 18 year period. There were two minimal peaks in the totals firstly in 1994 and then again 2006, where the number of deaths reached 5,840. Lowest points were in 2002 where the numbers dipped to 5,534 and then 2008 where they dropped to 5,214. They reduced further in 2009 but then rose slightly to finish at 4,690.

Overall numbers of fatalities fluctueted though there is a minimal increase in the final year.
(157 words)

Grade: 7

Comment: The information is presented well. It is ordered properly and a good level of detail is included. Assertions are backed up with some facts and numbers. Some key words have spelling errors; there are a few incorrect verb forms.

Task 2

Some people thinking workers should work for 3 or 4 days only and not for 5 or 6 days. There are some different reasons why this is a good idea and I beleive such proposals are useful to help with society in general. First of all if people working only 3 or 4 days, employment figures will improve because companies will need to take on a bigger number of workers and this will beneficial to the employment statistics. Second this will be helpful to work and life balance. Many people working very hard and don't have time for their own lifes. They have not enough time for their family and for their own hobbies and interest. This is a disadvantage solved with less working. Finally the companies will have a bigger number of experts for working. So they can also benefit. In conclusion I agree that work for 3 or 4 days is better system.

Grade: 4

Comment: Clearly this answer is underlength so will immediately lose marks. In addition, it is not paragraphed, another error which would have been easy to avoid. The ideas expressed are appropriate and sensible. Some of the vocabulary is well chosen and shows range. But there are spelling mistakes and problems with grammar and word order throughout. Combined with the very obvious problems with length and paragraphing this reduces the overall grade.

Practice Test 8

Task 1

The bar chart provides informations about voluntary work completed by people from different types of family for sports in 2010. The pie chart is showing the type of work done by such volunteers during same period. In general, the percentage of volunteers working in sports was higher in families of two parents with children.

The percentage of volunteers for sports organisations was lowest from one parent families; only 10.9 per cent of this were working in sports. Volunteers from families of couples with children reached a much higher rate at 49.8 per cent. The percentage of volunteers from families of couples without children was over double that of one parent families, reaching 26.9 per cent.

The majority of volunteers working at sports organizations took on a teaching role, e.g. teaching, coaching, instructing. Over 200 000 volunteers did this types of job. The smallest number of people, less than half the numbers of teachers at just under 63 000, have worked in medical support. Approximately 158 000 volunteers do administrative or committee jobs and is the second biggest area for volunteers.

In summary, there were less volunteers working in sports from one-parent households; of those who did so, the majority volunteered to teach, coach or instruct. *(202 words)*

Grade: 6

Comment: The answer is reasonably comprehensive and includes information from both data sets. There are some errors with tense and verb forms which create a lack of flow and the same with some of the referencing and word formation. In places the supporting evidence does not include any data from the charts. But overall the answer is well organized, makes sense and some detail is included.

Task 2

Sports stars are as famous as film stars nowadays. They have an increasingly prominent role with the media and earn large amounts of money; but this can create mixed reactions. For some people sports stars are deserving, positive role models; for others, the increasing amounts of money and media attention are damaging. It is useful to consider both viewpoints before making a decision in the matter.

One common argument is that high financial and social rewards encourages younger people to become interested in sports. Whilst not everyone will become rich and famous, any trend supports people in doing more sport should be seen as a good thing. On the other hand, it is possible that people might become fascinated by sports for the wrong reasons and it will attract those more interested in money or fame than actual sports. For example, it can give young people unrealistic expectations and stop them working towards more achievable goals.

Another argument in favour of sports people earning substantail money and media attention is that it makes sports more exciting. However, this diverts attention from the real focus of compitition and into making a profit. In other words it could be claimed that team loyalty and enthusiasm for the sport itself have disappeared as money has become too important.

Finally, some assert that sports people can only be at the top of their career for a limited number of years so they should be able to exploit every opportunity. But this should not be the main motivation and this could be argued to some degree about anyone in a job requiring physical fitness.

It is unlikely that the fame and money earned by sports people will reduce any time soon but this trend of more money and attention is not beneficial to sports overall. *(302 words)*

Grade: 8

Comment: The structure of the essay is sensible and each point is related to the question. The writer balances the arguments before coming to a final conclusion. Grammar is well controlled but there are a few minor errors. There are also a couple of spelling errors.

Sample answers

Task 1

The bar chart demonstrate the proportion of people, by gender, who were arrested for a variety of crime in 2008, 2009 – there are a number of clear trends visibal.

Firstly it is clear that number of males arrested outweighing the number of women in most case except violent against a person and theft or handling stolen goods. In these two categories, females outnumbered men approximately 2 per cent in the former category and around 20 per cent in the later category. More people arrested for these types of crime than any others for both genders.

Over 30 per cent of men arrested for violence; however only about 2 per cent of men arrested for fraud and forgery. In comparison about 34 per cent of women arrested for violence and only about 1 per cent of women arrested for robbery.

Overall more men than women arrested for different types of crime; higher numbers of both genders were for violence and for theft while lower numbers arrested for fraud and for robbery. *(170 words)*

Grade: 5

Comment: The answer contains factual errors – the number of women arrested is higher in three, not two, categories. Passives are used incorrectly all the time and there are other errors which make it difficult to read.

Task 2

Pensioners are some of the most vulnerabel people in our society and many old people live on very small amounts of money earned through a pension. It is arguable that the state should do more to help retired people. Nevertheless, if such provision is not available then workers have to be realist and prepare for their own retirement.

One way that this will happen is if people will be given support to do this. When they are at work, people should be offered bonus schemes which should allow them to save up for their retirement. Governments can offer tax deductions, for example, which will be help people to save. There is a possibile that workers may still try to avoid paying into a pension because life is expensive and some people don't have enough money for day to day life. But at least this will offer more possibile of saving.

Another solution is that the government could offer proper education. Many people have no idea where to start if they asked about retirement plans so it is likely that some lessons or advice on how to invest can be useful. These lessons should be available for older people not those at school although financial planning for school leavers is also a good idea. Of course some people will still not plan their pension despite education but at least the tools will have offered.

Finally I think there should be some benefits to help poor people like credits they could add to their pension if they don't have enough money. Not everyone is rich enough to put money away each month and this should be recognized.

Overall I believe that a mixture of tax breaks, education and support will help the government to encourage people to plan for retire. *(298 words)*

Grade: 6

Comment: The answer is developed well and has sensible paragraphing. Some parts of the writing are quite ambitious but the grammar is not very well controlled. The sentences are generally understandable but there are problems with conditionals and other forms.

Practice Test 10

Task 1

The pie chart provides a breakdown of the types of language used by those on the internet by the end of 2001 and the table offers information about the number of people using the net as a percentage of the world's population.

[handwritten: internet]

The percentage of the global population increased year on year for the given period, reaching its highest level in 2001. At this point 8.4 per cent of the world's population was online, a surprisingly low number but still much higher than the figure in 1997, which was a mere 1.8 per cent. In the years between 1999 and 2001 the percentage of internet users had almost doubled from 4.6 to 8.4 per cent overall.

Of these users the majority, a huge 43 per cent of the total, used English online. Use of English outstripped all the other languages, the next most popular of which was Japanese at 8.9 per cent. Chinese was just behind at 8.8 per cent and German and Spanish were the next most frequent at 6.8 and 6.5 per cent respectively. The other languages, including Korean, Italian and French, largely reached 3 or 4 per cent at most.

In summary, as the percentage of the world's population comes online, by far the biggest number will be using English to do so. *(201 words)*

[handwritten: not sure why so it should be ok this prediction]

Grade: 9

Comment: The data has been chosen appropriately with the key facts identified and described, so content is solid. The range of grammar and vocabulary is wide but also used accurately. Spelling and punctuation are accurate. There is a clear summary.

Task 2

In today's cosmopolitan world it is unusual to find a major city or country where there are no immigrants. People travel more now than they ever did in the past and populations have had to adapt to this transitional lifestyle much more quickly than in the past. Ultimately society, as a group of individuals, directs the way that new arrivals in a country are treated. But the government can do a number of things to support this.

Firstly, all governments should insist that schools teach history and culture from more than one country, not just the home nation. By learning how others have lived we gain insight into alternative cultures and ways of life which makes us more accepting when we meet people from those countries. Of course we don't have time to learn about the history of every country in the world but understanding at least one other culture opens our minds and makes us more tolerant.

In addition, when immigrants choose to settle in a country, the host government should offer free language and culture lessons. It is impossible for new arrivals to integrate if they do not understand the language and habits of their new home. I believe it is important for immigrants to learn the culture of the place they have chosen to settle. By acquiring the language and knowledge about the culture, they will be able integrate more easily and comfortably without necessarily losing their own identity.

Finally the governments of countries should make sure that they have some stringent laws to protect people from aggression or prejudice so that, should an immigrant face terrible attitudes, they have some protection. By ensuring people feel safe the host country shows that it is civilized and promotes integration.

In summary, understanding others is the key to harmonious living but laws should also be in place to protect people from those who can't behave responsibly. *(317 words)*

Grade: 9

Comment: There are a number of well-defined points made which are relevant and answer the question. The introduction and conclusion are clearly written and overall structure is managed effectively, with a good flow. Paragraphs are arranged logically and sentences linked smoothly. Grammar and vocabulary are sophisticated and error free. The range and accuracy of language and the full answer mean this is level 9.

Answer Key

Unit 1

Task 1

1
1g   2d   3b   4e   5a   6c   7f

2
Students' own answers.

3
a 15-year-old children with poor/low/ bad levels of literacy/reading and writing
b 4
c 2000, 2003, 2006, 2009

4
a Y = vertical axis, X = horizontal axis
b 1b   2a

5
a 3   b 1
c consistently higher = Austria, consistently lower = Denmark
d All the countries finished at a higher level by the end except one. Ireland generally has the lowest level throughout except right at the end. Austria generally has the highest level throughout except at the beginning.
e It shows the trends very clearly over time.

6
a 20 minutes
b Minimum 150 words

7
1d   2c   3b   4a

8
a the number of people taking different courses in China
b numbers in millions/years

9
a three upward, one with a downward dip in 2010
b the line for undergraduate courses is consistently higher throughout, the line for literacy courses is consistently lower throughout

c Undergraduate courses have the highest uptake and online courses the second highest uptake at both the beginning and the end of the period. However, both finish at higher levels by the end. At the beginning, postgraduate and literacy courses have roughly similar numbers but by the end postgraduate courses have slightly more people enrolled.

10
Possible answers

1 Introduction	*Data identified – 4 types of course in China Dates specified – 2008–2012*
2 Downward trends	Literacy course fell from 1.5 million (08) to nearly 0 (2010). Lowest overall. Rose slightly at end to about 1 million.
3 Upward trends	Undergraduate courses – rose from 19 to 23 million (2008/2012). Postgraduate numbers rose slightly from 1.5 million to just above 2 million. Online training rose from around 3.5 million (2008) to 5 million (2010).
4 Overview	Final summary: All courses showed an upward trend except literacy – slight dip. Undergraduate courses higher throughout.

11
c, a, d, b

12
a downward trend, dipping to, rose
b gradually
c demonstrates
d increased steadily, upward trend

13
a pie chart   b table   c bar chart
d process diagram

14
a b and c
b a shows percentages/proportions; d shows a process or procedure
c a
d c

Task 2

1
a students using technology to learn
b women learning traditionally 'male' subjects

2
Students' own answers.

3
1d   2a   3c   4b

4

Measures	Opinion	Benefit	Causes
channels	attitude	*advantage*	effect
methods	disagreement	difficulty	reasons
procedures	opposition	drawback	roots
steps	point of view	hindrance	sources

5
Contrasting viewpoints essay = opinion/benefit columns
Evaluation and opinion essay = opinion/benefit columns
Problem-solving essay = causes/ measures columns

6
a benefits/advantages, difficulties/ drawbacks/hindrances
b reasons/causes, steps/measures
c points of view/attitudes/opinions
d reasons, effect

7
a a minimum of 250 words
b 40 minutes
c This will not leave enough time for the other task, you will be marked down if you write too much.
d evaluation and opinion, *To what extent do you agree?*
e Education for those who pay, government should not fund people

8
a introducing topic   b stating opinion   c/d justifying opinion
e summarizing point of view

9
1 Firstly 2 Furthermore 3 also
4 In conclusion

Unit 2

Task 1

1
2 hacker   3/4 domain/traffic
5/6 app/device   7/8 state-of-the-art/obsolete

2
Students' own answers.

3
Possible answers:
b Mobile apps are downloadable tools and/which are often free.
c The cloud, a storage environment not reliant on a PC, is a virtual internet space/space on the internet.
d The first French-based technical website/web page went online in 1991.
e Instant messaging, an enhanced real-time mode of communication, allows quick transmission of text.
f Smart phones, one of the biggest selling technological devices available, have a wide variety of applications.

4
Possible answers:
Poland has highest levels most of the time, Mexico the next highest (overtaking Poland in one month only).
Togo has lowest numbers throughout.
Turkey's numbers consistently rise; Poland's numbers go down. The numbers of the other three countries fluctuate.

5
1 draws   2 style, each
3 in summary   4 slipped   5 peaked

6/7

Verbs showing downward movement	Verbs showing upward movement	Verbs showing little or no movement
slipped	climbed	hold (steady at)
fall fell	increased	level (off)
dipped	peaked	range
decline	go up	reach
decrease	grow (to)	remain (stable at)
drop	rise	span
go down	soar	stay (constant at)
plunge		
slump		

8
1b, dramatically   2c, steeply
3a, slightly

9
1c   2d   3b

10
graph 1: a and b (any order) gradually, marginally, moderately, modestly, progressively, slightly, steadily
graph 2: c and d (any order) dramatically, markedly, noticeably, sharply, significantly

11
a

b

12
a verb + adverb   b *there is/was* + adjective + noun

13
a In Turkey there was a steady increase in numbers from 47 in 2003 to over double that in 2007.
b Poland's numbers fell slightly to 226 in 2007.
c From 2005 to 2006 Mexican numbers dropped steeply to 179.
d Finally there was a slight rise, ending at a total of 183.

14
Possible answer:
Numbers fell slightly from 103 in 2003 to 92 in 2004. There was another slight fall to 89 in 2005. There was a modest rise to 97 in 2006.

Task 2

1
a children spending too much time online   b antisocial behaviour due to the internet   c fraud through online crime

2
Possible answers:
a speed and ease of access/ addiction to net
b improves research skills/ overreliance on the internet
c helps people who are shy or who live in remote places/not 'real' face-to-face life
d can work anywhere/can't escape work

3
Students' own answers.

4
Yes, Undoubtedly/Obviously/ Inevitably/Naturally/Shockingly/ Sadly/Interestingly/Realistically

5
Group 1: Implies the writer thinks everyone agrees/it is general knowledge.
Group 2: Implies the writer thinks this is a bad thing.
Group 3: Shows the writer considers the idea important.
Group 4: Shows the writer is making an assumption.

6
1B   2C   3A   4 D

7
Possible answers:
1a Generally speaking
1b Inevitably/Obviously
1c Unfortunately   2a Clearly/ Obviously   2b Worryingly
2c   Importantly/Significantly
3a Shockingly   3b Without doubt/ Undoubtedly   3c By and large

8
theory-based essay

9
Students' own answers.

10
Students' own answers.

11
I therefore agree that, actually, obviously, ironically, Unfortunately, clearly, I would argue that

12
d, e, c, b, a

13
1b 2d 3a 4b 5c 6b 7e
8c 9d 10c 11e 12a

14
b1 a2 c3 d4

15
1b 2c 3a

Unit 3

Task 1

1
Places: attraction, baggage reclaim, harbour, heritage site, resort, untouched destinations
People and characteristics: domestic visitor, guide, have itchy feet, have the travel bug, passenger, tourist
Types of journey: backpacking trip, cruise, package tour, trip, voyage, weekend break

2
Students' own answers.

3
Students' own answers.

4
a a potentially popular resort
b contemporary city   c visit it/ Cancun each year

5
a The sentences in the text use the passive voice.
b Because it is not clear/it is not important who is doing the action. The emphasis is on the action, not the subject.

6
a was identified as a potentially popular resort
b became a success/a successful resort
c it was/became successful

7
1 As a result of   2 Due to
3 Because of   4 as a consequence
5 meant that   6 for this reason

8
1d 2b 3e 4f 5c 6g 7a

9
b gets   c goes   e is inspected, is made

10
a for this reason, due to   e as a consequence of   f because, therefore
g because of this

11
a In this final phase   b First of all
c then   d (no signposting language)
e The next stage
f/g (no signposting language)

12
Opening stages: first of all, in the first stage
Middle stages: then, the next stage, after this, next, subsequently
Final stages: in this final stage, at the end, in the last stage

13

Possible answer:
The diagram illustrates the way that a small holiday resort can change to a larger one. At the first stage, new hotels are set up in the resort to meet the needs of tourists and as a result more jobs are created in the hotels themselves. Local businesses can then supply services to the new hotels, and other companies are also attracted to the area, which in turn creates more jobs. Subsequently, local workers can spend more freely as a reliable job ensures they have a stable source of income, which they spend in the area. This prosperous environment also increases the popularity of the resort, bringing in even more business. More jobs also mean more tax and income for the area in general. This additional revenue allows the local government to arrange for improvements in infrastructure and local facilities, meaning that the resort is even more attractive to tourists. As the resort becomes more popular, companies earn higher profits, which can be used for reinvestment. In the final stage, the added appeal leads to the need for further hotels and more of them are built.

Task 2

1
Europe, Because tourism affects the economic position of a country.

2
a8 b7 c1 d2 e3 f4 g5 h6

3
a noun 'of' noun: (a), d, e
b noun in object position: a, b
c compound noun: c, f, g
d noun phrase with preposition: a, d, e, h

4
the replacement

5
1 (Levels) of tourism coming to a host country are a key factor in the improvement of/in improving the (economy) of (the host country).
2 (The tour guide was particularly bad because she had) no capacity to organize/for organizing (the group).
3 Beach resorts (are popular for relaxing holidays).
4 (Some) local communities become reliant upon tourism (income).

6
benefits of tourism, problems it creates, Discuss both views, give your own opinion. Yes.

7
Students' own answers.

8
Students' own answers.

9
At first glance, tourism seems to be a huge advantage for the local area.   Nevertheless, the assumption that tourism is always a benefit is increasingly under fire.

10
1a 2b 3a 4a 5b 6a 7a 8b

11
1b 2e 3d 4c 5f 6a

12
A commonly held view is that tourism is a huge advantage for the local area./Although there is some truth to these ideas it is also true to say that there are some disadvantages, too.

13

Possible answer:

Idea two
It seems a fair suggestion that tourism can also improve infrastructure. Obviously, the need to provide good facilities and transportation for visitors to encourage them to spend money in the area means some priority is given to this. The benefits are also felt by the local population. However, this makes the assumption that development is always positive whereas sometimes it results in damage to the environment and is not sustainable in the long term. For example, beautiful areas could get overdeveloped.

Idea three

An argument that is often made is that tourism brings many benefits such as a new population looking for work and an increase in attractions and facilities. Clearly if there are many tourists in the area, it is likely that there will be a growth in cafes, restaurants and so on. Although sympathetic to the advantages that tourism brings, I also believe that such developments can create problems. The history and character of an area can change or get lost as the environment becomes increasingly commercialized.

Unit 4

Task 1

1

Possible answer:
opera/ballet/art/classical music concert are likely to be high culture breakdancing and graffiti are likely to be low culture

2

Students' own answers.

3

Possible answers:
streaming opera to cinemas, access to free online concerts

4

Students' own answers.

5

1 A male   B female
2 i) pop Table 2   ii) opera Table 3
   iii) classical music Table 1

6

1d   2a   3e   4c   5b   6f

7

1 countable nouns, noun
2 uncountable nouns, noun
3 adjectives, adjective   4 adjectives, adjective   5 similarity   6 slightly
7 considerably, far, significantly, substantially

8

Rule 1: a, b, c, 2, 4, 5
Rule 2: d
Rule 3: f, 6
Rule 4: e, 3
Rule 5: 1
Rule 6: d
Rule 7: b, c, 7

9

Possible answers:

1 The percentage of those aged 18 to 24 using their smartphones to watch television was much higher than for any other group.
2 The 35-to-44 age group used their phones substantially more than those in the 55-to-64 age group.
3 The group with the fewest number of people using their phones for this purpose was the 65+ category.
4 Slightly more people in the 18-to-24 age group use their phones to watch TV compared to the 25-to-34 age group.
5 Those in the 55-to-64-year-old age group use their phones to stream television much less than those in the 25-to-34-year-old group.

10

1 18, 24   2 65+   3 45, 54   4 55, 64   5 25, 34

11

Possible answers:

1 vast majority   2 roughly   3 with the lowest number of   4 Just below/Slightly below   5 double   6 much higher   7 just over

12

1 in contrast   2 compared to
3 whereas

13

a whilst/while 3   b conversely/on the other hand 1   c in comparison with 2

14

Contrast: 1 whereas   2 while
3 whilst   4 in contrast
Concession: 5 although   6 though
7 despite   8 in spite of   9 However
10 Nevertheless

15

1 while/whereas/whilst   2 although/though   3 In contrast   4 Despite/In spite of   5 However/Nevertheless

Task 2

1

art gallery or museum: abstract, curator, exhibit, painting, portrait, sculpture
cinema: aisle, box office, film script, projector, screen, usher
music concert: gig, microphones, speakers, stage, support act, vocalist
theatre: aisle, box office, curtain, play, stage, usher

2

Students' own answers.

3

Possible answers

1 problematic/disadvantageous
2 beneficial   3 advantageous
4 useful 5 difficult/problematic/disadvantageous

4

2 If programmes are of good quality, TV can be beneficial (to children).
3 If extra income from entrance fees is possible, museums that charge will be in an advantageous position.
4 If we censor films and TV programmes, it will ensure they are useful (and do not harm the development of children).
5 If the general public continue to download films and music illegally, without paying, financing future productions will be difficult.

5

1 Unless, Providing that, On condition that, We should, Should
2 unless

6

Suggest solutions.

7

Suggestion 1 Museums provide free entry	Advantage: could encourage more people to visit and get them interested at a younger age Disadvantage: loss of income
Suggestion 2 More interactive exhibitions	Advantage: more accessible to younger people Disadvantage: expensive to manage
Suggestion 3 Good advertising	Advantage: reminds people of what is there, increases numbers Disadvantage: could attract inappropriate people/crowds

8

Firstly, In addition, Lastly

9

1 Furthermore a   2 To conclude c
3 In summary c   4 Moreover a
5 As well as this/that a

10

Unless there are sufficient visitors at museums, maintaining them will be problematic…; it would be useful if museums could provide free entry; if we take the view that culture should be available to everyone, it is logical to suggest that the government should fund each museum. If entry was free, this would immediately encourage more people to go…; if funds could be provided centrally, this wouldn't be a problem.

… provided that it doesn't harm any of the exhibits, more interactive exhibitions would encourage younger people to go to museums.

If some interactive activities such as screen-based games were available, it would make the museum accessible to younger visitors.

Unless museums advertise, people won't be aware of what they can offer.

There are three patterns (*unless*, *if*, *provided that*).

11

It would make the statements stronger (*will*) or less likely (*could*).

Unit 5

Task 1

1

Students' own answers.

2

Students' own answers.

3

1d   2e   3b   4a   5c

4

1 construction of houses   2 elderly generation   3 urban growth
4 conservation areas
5 overpopulation

5

Students' own answers.

6

Possible answer:
2 likely to be: past/present/future forms

7

1 The first sentence is present perfect as it describes a trend that covers the past up to the present time.
2 At that time it <u>was</u> at a level of just under 1 billion people and <u>rose</u> gradually until the year 2000 when the number of people living in cities <u>was</u> roughly double its previous level.
3 It <u>is</u> still <u>increasing</u> now and <u>has been growing</u> more rapidly since 2005 when it overtook rural population levels. (Present continuous – talking about what is happening currently; present perfect continuous – talking about what has happened between the past and now.)
4 The numbers of city dwellers <u>are predicted to</u> rise further and it <u>is projected</u> that they <u>will</u> reach just under 5 billion by 2030. (Present simple passive for prediction; *will* for the future – again a prediction.)

8

Time expression	Tense	Example
since 1950	present perfect	*The urban population of the world has risen steadily*
at that time	past simple	*it was at a level of just under 1 billion people, and rose*
the year 2000	past simple	*the number of people living in cities was roughly double its previous level*
now	present continuous	*It is still increasing*
since 2005	present perfect continuous	*has been growing more rapidly since 2005*
by 2030	*will* for future	*they will reach just under 5 billion by 2030*

9

a The numbers of city dwellers are likely to rise further and it is expected that they will reach just under 5 billion by 2030.
b The numbers of city dwellers are set to rise further and it is forecast that they will reach just under 5 billion by 2030.

10

1 has followed   2 began
3 increased   4 reached   5 was maintained   6 has fallen   7 is predicted   8 is projected   9 will drop

11

1b   2c   3a   4c   5c   6d   7a   8d
9d   10d   11a   12c

12

Possible answers:
1 The populations of all four countries rose strongly between 1950 and 1960.
2 The populations of India and China increased steeply between 1950 and 2010, with India reaching 1.2 billion and China achieving numbers slightly higher at 1.3 billion.
3 The population of the USA showed a slight rise to around 300 million.
4 Europe's figures went up marginally from 500 million to roughly 650 million between 1950 and 1990 then levelled off, showing little further increase.
5 The USA and Europe's figures are currently levelling off or dropping in comparison to China and India, where figures are still climbing.
6 China and India are expected to achieve populations of 1.35 billion 1.5 billion respectively.
7 Europe and the USA are projected to increase their populations gradually with the USA increasing its population by roughly three quarters to just over 400 million, and Europe's population dipping very slightly to reach 650 million.

Task 2

1

1a   2d   3b, c   4b   5b, c

2

Students' own answers.

3

Problem-solving

4
2c 5a 7e 9b 11d
5
Opinion held by writer
I partly agree that space needs to be used well.
Agree space is important but not the only factor to consider.
Generally accepted opinion
Cities: have high density of buildings. Important to use space effectively – population of world increasing/ more people need to live in cities
Design of high-rise architecture suitable for buildings in city – buildings in cities generally contemporary and high rise – economic use of space.
Attractive surroundings improve quality of life/attract tourists and income
Nowadays good design includes green space but still economic – also better for environment
6
It is generally accepted that, it is therefore commonly acknowledged that, I would therefore maintain that, Experts claim that, For this reason, I believe, It seems to me that
7

Personal opinion	Impersonal idea
I would therefore maintain that For this reason, I believe It seems to me that	It is generally accepted that It is therefore commonly acknowledged that Experts claim that

8

Personal opinion	Impersonal idea
I think In my opinion To my mind As far as I'm concerned Personally, I am certain I feel (that)	It should be noted that It is claimed that Many might claim Reports show/state/ demonstrate/ reveal that A general assertion is Predictions suggest that

9
1c 2a 3d 4e 5b 6f
10
Students' own answers.
11
1d, e 2f 3c 4a, b
12
1 such as 2 A case in point is 3 In other words/That is to say 4 that is to say/in other words/for example/for instance 5 for example/instance

Unit 6

Task 1
1
Students' own answers.
2
Students' own answers.
3
Students' own answers.
4
a fast/junk food, comfort, confectionery, convenience, delicious, savoury (also possible: macrobiotic, (un)healthy)
b balanced, crash, obesity, macrobiotic, sensible, starvation, (un)healthy
c factory farming, free-range, intensive farming, organic farming, pesticides, sustainable agriculture
5
1 greenhouse 2 sorting
3 peeling/polishing 4 cutting
5 chilling 6 spinning/drying
7 packaging
6
1
a iv b i c ii d iii
2
Having been collected, …
3
The first stage, subsequently, then, Next, After this, Finally
7
1 in order to 2 so as to 3 for
4 to 5 so that 6 in order that
8
expressing purpose
9
1 in order to 2 so as to 3 to
4 for 5 so that 6 in order that
10
1b 2c 3d 4e 5a

11
Possible answers:
1
The flow chart demonstrates the production of bread dough.
2
a The process involves mixing a number of ingredients including yeast, flour and water and some additives for fermentation.
b There are three key stages, beginning with a mixing stage, followed by a fermentation stage and finishing with the dough being divided.
3
a The ingredients are put into the mixer in order to combine them.
b Additives are put in the mix so as to ferment it.
c The dough is put into a divider to divide it into smaller pieces of equal size.
4
The process involves mixing a number of ingredients including yeast, flour and water and some additives for fermentation. There are three key stages, beginning with a mixing stage, followed by a fermentation stage and finishing with the dough being divided. In the first stage the ingredients are put into the mixer in order to combine them. Once this is done, additives are added to the mixture so as to ferment it. Finally, the fermented dough is put into a divider to create small pieces of equal size. These can then be baked to create loaves of bread.

Task 2
1
Students' own answers.
2
Possible answers:
1 Deforestation causes soil erosion because there is less vegetation to protect the soil. This results in poor quality soil and food production is therefore damaged.

2 Global warming creates higher temperatures and this impacts on the climate. Rainfall becomes unreliable and farmers find there are periods where there is not enough rain, followed by periods when there is so much it causes floods. Either of these means that the crops are damaged or cannot grow properly.

3 During war, farmers can't work on their land because it is too dangerous or what crops they have are damaged by fighting or taken by the army. This means food production drops. But also the war disrupts transport of imports or exports so food can't be brought in and exports don't raise money.

4 High prices reduce demand for food and make what is there difficult for poor people to buy. Consequently, there is less available food for people and they starve.

3

1 *wholefoods*: food that does not contain artificial substances

2 *chemical fertilizers*: a chemical substance added to soil to help make plants grow

3 *Genetically modified*: Genetically modified crops have their genetic structure changed to make them more suitable for a specific purpose.

4 *Overgrazing* and *deforestation*: Overgrazing is where animals are allowed to eat too much grass from fields so that the land is damaged; deforestation is the process of removing trees from an area.

5 *climate change*: The changes thought to be affecting the world's weather, making it warmer/colder/less predictable.

4

Students' own answers.

5

a As wholefoods are healthier than other foods, eating natural produce is important for me.

b Eating natural produce is important for me because wholefoods are healthier than others.

c Since wholefoods and natural produce are healthier than other types, eating them is important for me.

6

Possible answers:

2 Since intensive farming increases the use of pesticides and chemical fertilizers, I prefer to shop at a farmers' market where the food is usually locally produced and organic.

3 As genetically modified crops help to prevent starvation, producing much greater quantities of crops, they are crucial.

4 Overgrazing and deforestation mean there is less food production so farmers and landowners should be banned from allowing this.

5 Developed countries should focus on solutions for climate change as this issue impacts heavily on food production in developing countries.

7

evaluate a solution

8

Introduction: b, c, a, d
Conclusion: d, c, b, a

9

Suggested solution, advantages, disadvantages

10

repetitiveness

11

1b   2e   3g   4c   5d   6f   7a

12

1d   2a   3d   4f   5c   6e   7e

13

alternative solution

14

it = famine   it = famine   Such = resources are spent on weapons or armies   their = farmers   these = having control over unstable political systems and influence over the processes of war   this = having control over unstable political systems and influence over the processes of war

15

1 It/This   2 it   3 these/such
4 their   5 Such an/This   6 the

16

Possible answer:

The difficulty with technology as a solution is that it requires economic investment. Of course this is possible in a limited way. Such money for water pumps and similar can be raised through charity but this will not be sufficient on its own. However, of all the solutions this one is the most viable immediately.

Unit 7

Task 1

1

Students' own answers.

2

a *workshy*   b work mates
c working week   d shift work
e workload   f workplace   g working age   h Hard work/Working hard

3

Students' own answers.

4

Job: apply for, high-powered, hold down, manual, permanent, safeguard, satisfaction, skilled
Salary: annual, competitive, full, final, high, increase, safeguard, starting

5

Students' own answers.

6

1 permanent job/high or annual salary   2 applied for   3 manual jobs   4 high-powered job   5 job satisfaction   6 permanent job/competitive salary

7

1 Not having income   2 Arriving at the office,   3 leaving many of those doing manual jobs   4 Given enough time, 5 enjoying the job satisfaction, 6 Before getting a more permanent job/competitive salary

8

a1   b4   c3   d2   e5   f6

9

1 Sentence b is in the past. The main verb tells us this.

2 Sentence b emphasises the order of the actions.

3 a is active, b is passive

10

a Getting/Having got such excellent qualifications, she didn't have problems getting her first job.
b After graduating, he spent some time on a gap year.
c My manager, having just given in his notice, wants me to leave too and work with him.
d Providing the job is completed step by step, it won't be difficult.
e Having offered a lot of help, the teacher encouraged her student to work autonomously.

11

Possible answers:
There is a predicted overall reduction in the number of people in work per pensioner.
The lowest number of people in work per pensioner is predicted to be in 2033 where it drops to just over 2.7. The highest number is likely to be in 2019 where it is approximately 3.26. The steepest fall is from around 2026 to 2034.
There is a slight increase which began in 2010 and is likely to continue until approximately 2019.

12

Students' own answers.

13

Possible answers:
1 making   2 hitting   3 rising
4 (After) having reached/After reaching/Having reached

14

bar

15

unless, without

16

1 All the quantities are fractions except for d, which is a percentage.
2 None of the examples are whole numbers other than c (which is a whole/single number).
3 The quantities are all much lower than 20 with the exception of a (which is only slightly less/only a little less).
4 The quantities are all related in amount bar c (which is more general).

17

Students' own answers.

Task 2

1
Students' own answers.

2
1 No, because this is 'claimed' and the statistics are 'not exact' and can be 'refuted'.
2 Not good – they often experience hazardous conditions or suffer cruelty.
3 22 000 children die in work-related accidents each year.
4 There is no legal protection for many children.

3
Students' own answers.

4
Inversion of adjective, verb and subject.

5
1b   2d   3c   4a

6
1 So high is the amount of time spent by people at work that they often suffer from stress-related illnesses.
2 Standing at the front of the meeting, the manager announced some redundancies.
3 So satisfied are employees with the opportunities to progress in the company that they don't leave.
4 Much more exciting than his previous role in banking was (his job in) social work.
5 Badly paid it might be, but the job provides a high level of job satisfaction.

7
a claim, slave-like conditions
b suggests   c can be refuted
d seems, convincing evidence

8
Verbs: claim, suggests, can be refuted, seems
Adjective + noun forms: slave-like conditions, convincing evidence
All verbs are used actively except *refuted*, which is used passively

9/10

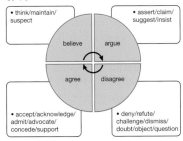

- think/maintain/suspect
- assert/claim/suggest/insist
- believe
- argue
- agree
- disagree
- accept/acknowledge/admit/advocate/concede/support
- deny/refute/challenge/dismiss/doubt/object/question

11
a conceded   b refused   c proof
d debatable   e reasoned evidence
f unclear   g source   h item
i ailment   j heavy

12
assert, object, maintaining

13
Students' own answers.

14
Students' own answers.

15
Students' own answers.

Unit 8

Task 1

1
Students' own answers.

2
a beneficial, suffering   b committed, supporters   c useful, advice
d gradually, sufficient   e Excelling receive

3
Students' own answers.

4
a swimming   b football   c tennis
d golf

5
a goggles, pool   b goal, pitch
c court, racquet   d clubs, course

6
a rise in the summer months
b Higher temperatures coincide with more heat-related illness.
c There is a rise in temperature in July but illnesses do not peak until August. The increase in temperature is steady but the increase in illness is a sudden peak not a moderately gradual rise. There is a rise in heat-related illness in January but temperatures are very low.

7

Introduction: clarifies the type of information given in the two different data sets.

Paragraph 1: gives key information from data set one and identifies correlations between this and data from set 2.

Paragraph 2: looks at further key information from data set one and identifies where this doesn't correlate with the data in set 2.

Conclusion: provides a brief summary of the overall information and how closely it appears to be linked in each set of information.

8

a4 b1 c5 d2 e3

9

correlates with, proportional trends, the correlation is not consistent

10

1 both   2 strong   3 limited

11

a no relationship at all   b One trend negatively affects the other, i.e. when one goes up the other goes down.

Task 2

1

Students' own answers.

2

a tai chi   b cycling/mountain biking
c skateboarding   d yoga
Students' own answers for associations.

3

The debate is about age limit in sports, particularly the Olympics.
For: people are too old and will have more injuries.
Against: everyone has a right to compete.

4

Students' own answers.

5

Students' own answers.

6

Adjective	Verb	Noun
competitive	compete	competition
athletic	✗	athlete
knowledgeable	know	knowledge
believable	believe	belief
maintained	maintain	maintenance
accomplished	accomplish	accomplishment
distinct/ distinctive	distinguish	distinction
dominant/ dominating	dominate	domination
significant	signify	significance
important	✗	importance

7

1 competitive/dominant
2 accomplished/knowledgeable
3 important, knowledgeable
4 athletic/competitive   5 Belief

8

Students' own answers.

9

3

10

	Benefit	Drawback
Idea one	Learn how to work with others to succeed. d	For some people the only motivation is winning. a
Idea two	Encourages people to be resilient and support each other even when hard. b	Teaches people to be aggressive in order to achieve what they want. f
Idea three	People learn about losing as well as winning. c	Don't learn that some aspects of life are not competitive e

11

b It is important to learn how to work with other people, who may have ideas to help with success.

c A dominant idea is that being competitive encourages people to be resilient, which is important as sports are often challenging and require people to support each other.

d Significantly, sport teaches people to gain what they want by being aggressive, which is not a healthy approach in general.

12

a significant   b important
c dominant   d Significantly

13

1 Jogging is a sport ~~who~~ **which/ that** you can do with no special equipment.

2 Having a trainer who understand**s** about exercise can help you get fit more quickly.

3 The athlete, **who/having** won the world championship, has made a great deal of money.

4 His football career ended when he broke his leg, ~~that~~ **which** was crucial to his sporting ability.

5 The referee, who we depend **on** to keep the score, is not well today.

6 The games, none of ~~who~~ **which** they won, were well attended.

14

a True   b False (non-defining relative clauses give additional information)
c False ('that' can only be used for people in defining relative clauses)
d True   e False (dependent prepositions should be included)
f True

15

The second is more formal – the preposition is brought before the relative pronoun and *who* becomes *whom*.

16

a The sport, in which many people are interested, could not be accommodated in a centre big enough to run the competition.

b The final result, which everyone had agreed with, was nevertheless overruled by the referee.

c The game was watched by 25 000 people, a third of whom watched on digital TV.

d Teenagers, none of whom do much themselves, generally agree sport is healthy.

e Many participants in the survey, 23 per cent of whom went to the gym, did some kind of physical activity.

17

a a relative clause: those who see more extreme behaviour at football matches/any activity where participants sometimes behave badly

b a signposting noun: significance

18
a restate opinion 4
b summarize opposite viewpoint 2
c state opinion 1
d refute opposite viewpoint 3

19
To sum up, in general

20

Possible answer:
Ultimately, the Olympics are about sporting achievement and therefore I believe people should be allowed to compete whatever their age. It is vital that people are given the opportunity to show what they can do; the Olympics is a place where ability should surpass age, gender or other aspects of life that can hold people back.

Unit 9

Task 1

1
a social   b behaviour   c criminal
d hardened   e conviction
f previous   g rate

2
1a   2b   3b   4a   5a   6a   7b   8a

3
Students' own answers.

4
Students' own answers.

5
Students' own answers.

6/7
The pie chart illustrates the proportion of different crimes committed in **2011** (2010 to 2011), and includes **four** (five) different crime categories. In other words it looks at the rates of theft, burglary, vehicle-related crime, violent crime and vandalism. Theft made up the largest proportion at 35 per cent. This was three times as high as the rate for **burglary** (vehicle-related theft), which was a mere 12 per cent. The lowest proportion of offences related to **vehicle theft** (burglary) and this made up only 8 per cent of the total. Combined with vehicle theft, violent crime made up an equivalent proportion to theft in general, standing at 23 per cent on its own. That is to say, when added together they made up a total of 35 per cent.

Finally the **second** (third) highest proportion of crime was vandalism at 22 per cent.

8
In other words, That is to say

9
a spoken or written   b written
c spoken   d spoken   e written

10

Possible answers:
1 that is to say   2 in other words
3 To be more precise

11
The pie chart illustrates the proportion of different crimes committed in 2011, and includes five different crime categories. In other words it looks at the rates of theft, burglary, vehicle-related crime, violent crime and vandalism. Theft made up the largest proportion at 35 per cent. This was three times as high as the rate for burglary, which was a mere 12 per cent. The lowest proportion of offences related to vehicle theft and this made up only 8 per cent of the total. Combined with vehicle theft, violent crime made up an equivalent proportion to theft in general, standing at 23 per cent on its own. That is to say, when added together they made up a total of 35 per cent. Finally, the second highest proportion of crime was vandalism at 22 per cent.

12
a none   b none   c none   d the
e an   f the

13
1b   2e   3d   4c   5a

14
a –, the
b –, a or –, a, –, the, the
c The, –, –, –
d –, –, an, –, the
e –, the

Task 2

1

money	rich	poor
cash coins dough funding	affluent prosperous wealthy well off	broke destitute impoverished making ends meet

2
Formal: coins, funding, affluent, prosperous, wealthy, destitute, impoverished
Informal: cash, dough, well off, broke, making ends meet

3
Students' own answers.

4
Students' own answers.

5
1 China
2 through weight
3 The ease with which they could be transported.

6
1 fact   2 fact   3 opinion   4 opinion
5 fact

7
a3 b4 They are softened by additional phrases: *It seems that/It is probable that*

8
1 It appears that money brings out the worst in people.
2 Money possibly encourages people to work harder than they otherwise would.
3 There is a tendency for people to weaken their moral position if they think they can make a profit.
4 Occasionally we realize the extent to which materialism controls our life nowadays.

9
1 a appears   2 d Occasionally
3 c There is a tendency for
4 b possibly

10
a2   b4   c3   d1

11

Possible answers:
1 It seems that the banks have too much power.
2 It is probable that people need to get support …
3 Materialistic attitudes tend to be unhealthy.
4 It seems likely that there would be less crime …
5 If you are only motivated by money, you won't always be happy.

12
Problem-solving essay. Could be introduction, three ideas with the benefits and drawbacks of each highlighted, conclusion.

13

Students' own answers.

14

a1 b3 c2

15

Possible answer:

a The most important idea is to educate people in order that they can understand how to manage money. This would allow people to manage their finances much better. For this reason the government should provide lessons in school to help educate people so they can do this. One benefit of such a move would be that people will be more competent financially. However, this type of education would obviously take up time that some would claim could be better spent on other things, e.g. in schools time is often limited and is needed for other types of study.

b A further solution could be advisory centres which are able to offer free advice to people. The advantage is that this would help people before their problems became serious, in other words prevention rather than cure. On the other hand this might be quite expensive to run so would not be viable.

c Finally, banks and shops shouldn't lend to people who don't have enough money to meet their debts. This would immediately prevent people getting into trouble such as not having sufficient funds to manage a debt. The drawback to this is that it could cause hardship if people desperately need credit.

Unit 10

Task 1

1

1 ensure   2 predictable   3 address
4 generalize   5 miss out
6 paraphrase   7 analysing   8 key
9 state   10 range

2

1 check   2 foreseeable   3 tackle
4 make sweeping statements
5 omit   6 rephrase   7 evaluating
8 significant   9 express
10 selection

3

Students' own answers.

4

It suggests that the best age is as young as possible and there is some correlation between age and learning.

5

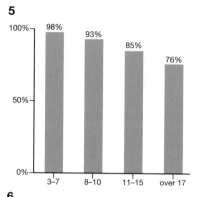

6

Aged 17 and over – the lowest scores on tests; aged 3–7 is the highest level.

7

Ordering ideas	Additions	Contrast	Concession
finally firstly next	also furthermore in addition to moreover subsequently	but on the other hand whereas while	however although despite nevertheless so long as unless
Showing reasons	**Showing result**	**Showing purpose**	**Exemplification**
as due to since	hence so therefore	in order to so as to to	for example for instance such as

8

Possible answers:

a Nevertheless,   b although/but
c As/Since   d Firstly   e hence/
therefore   f Despite   g In addition
to   h so as to/to/in order to
i such as   j but

Task 2

1

Students' own answers.

2

a4   b3   c1   d5   e2

3

1c   2a   3b

4

Possible answers:

1 Endangered languages in the world number 2 500 though some have less than 1 000 speakers.

2 Understanding your learning style is a good way to learn. You can identify the way that works best for you.

3 It is Mandarin Chinese and English which are the most spoken languages with Spanish being the third most common.

4 Learning a language is easier if it is similar to your own. Therefore a Polish speaker will find Slavic languages easier to learn than others.

5 Newly created artificial languages invented since the 17th century number 200. The best known is Esperanto with 2 million speakers.

5

a2   b3   c4   d1

6

1c   2a   3b   4d

7

a answers question 3, b answers question 1

8

a: no cohesion, basic sentences and vocabulary, lack of referencing
b: overuse of cohesion devices

	a	b
1 no clear introduction setting up the ideas	✓	
2 unclear planning – no central idea in each paragraph	✓	
3 basic sentences which lack variety	✓	
4 repetition of vocabulary	✓	
5 lack of cohesion or overuse of linkers	✓	✓
6 lack of referencing	✓	
7 poor grammar		
8 poor spelling		
9 unclear viewpoint or overgeneralized statements	✓	
10 no clear conclusion		

9

Possible answer:
Travel can be very beneficial to young people in many ways and therefore gap years, where students travel abroad for a time before embarking upon a career, can be very useful for people as they grow up. I would therefore maintain that travelling is a positive experience for young people.
Firstly, travelling allows people to broaden their minds by learning about an unknown culture. By spending time abroad the person will experience new and unique events and learn a great deal about the world around them. In general, this type of experience also helps people to develop their own personality as they begin to carve out their own opinions from a wider perspective.

10

Possible answer:
It is true to say that, even though the world is becoming increasingly globalized and international communication is important, people are still not learning a second language or learning enough about other cultures. Moreover, they don't think it is a disadvantage. There are a variety of solutions that might help with this problem.

11

a The number of people learning Chinese ~~are~~ **is** increasing.
b Many people ~~had~~ started to learn this to increase their employment prospects.
c ~~A~~ Culture is constantly changing as people travel the globe.
d Communication~~s~~ is important in maintaining good relations between countries.
e Due to this it is easier to learn a language.
f There is an increase in intercultural relationships and marriage ~~of~~ **with/to** a foreigner.
g The people ~~which~~ **who/that** have travelled are more open-minded.
h Being ~~well-travelling~~ **well-travelled** is a positive characteristic.

12
1e   2h   3a   4d   5g   6c   7b   8f

13
Travel can be very ~~benefit~~ **beneficial** to ~~the~~ young people in many ways and therefore gap years, ~~which~~ **where/when** ~~is~~ students travel abroad for a time before embarking upon a career, can be very useful for people as they grow up. I would therefore maintain that travelling ~~was~~ **is** a positive experience for young people.
First, travelling allows people to broaden their minds to ~~learning~~ **learn** about an unknown culture. And by spending time abroad the person will experience~~d~~ new and unique events. They can learn a great deal about the world around them. In general this type of experience also helps people to develop their own personality.~~-~~ ~~B~~ because they begin to carve out their own opinions from a wider perspective.
~~Also second~~ **Also/Secondly**, they can find **out** a lot about the rest of the world such as learning another language and meeting new people. This will make them ~~more~~ richer as a person when they eventually settle down and start to work~~ing~~. This must be a big advantag**e** and **will** give them a good start to working life. Finally they will have been learning responsibility and ~~autonomousness~~ **autonomy** because of their experience.
Therefore/For these reasons/All in all, I agree that people should try to travel after their studies finish.

MACMILLAN **EXAMS**

Written by leading IELTS author Sam McCarter, Direct to IELTS provides a short and concise course that combines print and online materials for a more interactive learning experience

- Bands 6.0 – 7.0

- Eight topic-based units cover the skills required for the academic module of the IELTS exam plus grammar and vocabulary build-up

- A 'Writing Bank' provides detailed and focused practice including all task types found in the writing exam and annotated model answers

- The website includes four computer-based practice tests, written by an experienced exam writer, as well as downloadable worksheets to accompany the Student's Book

WITH FOUR **ONLINE** PRACTICE TESTS

DIRECT TO

IELTS

Student's Book

Sam McCarter

MACMILLAN
EDUCATION

www.directtoielts.com

The IELTS Skills Apps

Exam practice exercises and interactive tasks to help you develop the skills you will need to excel in IELTS.

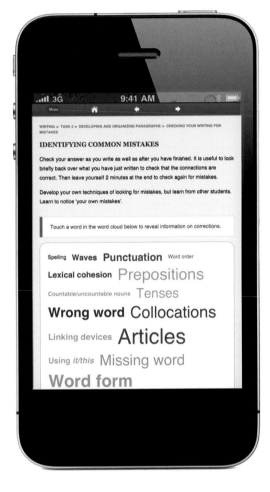

- Written by Sam McCarter, the author of the bestselling *Ready for IELTS* and *Tips for IELTS*
- Each skill is explained and comes with examples and an interactive exercise
- Practise answering the full range of question types that you can expect to find in the IELTS exam

- A detailed overview of the IELTS exam
- Score yourself on the interactive 'Can Do' statement section
- A wide range of innovative and interactive exercises that help you work on the essential skills needed for the IELTS exam

Learn more at the Macmillan Education Apps
website: www.macmillaneducationapps.com